Powerful Mind Through Self-Hypnosis

A Practical Guide to Complete Self-Mastery

First published by O-Books, 2010

O Books is an imprint of John Hunt Publishing Ltd., The Bothy, Deershot Lodge, Park Lane, Ropley,
Hants, SO24 0BE, UK
office1@o-books.net
www.o-books.com

Distribution in:	South Africa
	Stephan Phillips (pty) Ltd
UK and Europe	Email: orders@stephanphillips.com
Orca Book Services Ltd	Tel: 27 21 4489839 Telefax: 27 21 4479879
Home trade orders	Text copyright Cathal O'Briain 2010
tradeorders@orcabookservices.co.uk	
Tel: 01235 465521 Fax: 01235 465555	ISBN: 978 1 84694 298 3
Export orders	Design: Stuart Davies
exportorders@orcabookservices.co.uk	
Tel: 01235 465516 or 01235 465517	All rights reserved. Except for brief quotations
Fax: 01235 465555	in critical articles or reviews, no part of this
	book may be reproduced in any manner
USA and Canada	without prior written permission from the
NBN	publishers.
custserv@nbnbooks.com	
Tel: 1 800 462 6420 Fax: 1 800 338 4550	The rights of Cathal O'Briain as author have
	been asserted in accordance with the
Australia and New Zealand	Copyright, Designs and Patents Act 1988.
Brumby Books	
sales@brumbybooks.com.au	A CIP catalogue record for this book is
Tel: 61 3 9761 5535 Fax: 61 3 9761 7095	available from the British Library.
Far East (offices in Singapore, Thailand,	
Hong Kong, Taiwan)	
Pansing Distribution Pte Ltd	
kemal@pansing.com	
Tel: 65 6319 9939 Fax: 65 6462 5761	Printed in the UK by CPI Antony Rowe

We operate a distinctive and ethical publishing philosophy in all
areas of its business, from its global network of authors to
production and worldwide distribution.

Powerful Mind Through Self-Hypnosis

A Practical Guide to Complete Self-Mastery

Cathal O'Briain

BOOKS

Winchester, UK
Washington, USA

CONTENTS

Dedication

This book is dedicated to Jeff Gill. It was only when you were gone, I realized I had a best friend.

"The real you is emerging. The happy one. The peaceful one. The powerful one. A kindred spirit who is forever the learner, the observer. Neven shaken by fear, empowered by truth."

About the Author

Cathal O'Briain is a native of Dublin, Ireland and currently resides at his home and practice in County Kildare. He is a certified hypnotherapist, psychotherapist, and hypno-analyst. Cathal is also a member in good standing with the Institute of Clinical Hypnotherapy and Psychotherapy (IRL). His main areas of interest are hypnotherapy, psychoanalysis, mythology, and religion. In his capacity as Public Relations Officer and Speaker for the ICHP (named above), he frequently gives lectures in Self-Hypnosis and Analytical Psychotherapy at Marino College, Dublin. He also writes for their quarterly journal, *The Hypno Analyst*.

On completing second level education, Cathal began studying at Milltown Institute of Theology and Philosophy, where he hoped to get a taste of religious life. Taking classes in philosophy, and cognitive psychology, he savored his time there, but felt his Christian vocation lay elsewhere. Encouraged by a need to understand more about thinking, he then turned his attention to the study of hypnotherapy, art, and psychoanalysis. Cathal paid his way through college by working part time with physically challenged adults in the Richmond Cheshire Homes, Monkstown, Dublin. Much of his research there was centered on the effectiveness of self-hypnosis in easing muscular tension. Many of the young adults he worked with, some crippled with cerebral palsy and multiple sclerosis, found Cathal's hypnotic methods effective in relieving pain, and aiding sequential movement. Recalling his stay at the home, Cathal stressed that,

"In order for the physically disabled person to escape the additional burden of mental suffering, he or she must not become institutionalized. It is a reasonable speculation to see that a lack of activity outside of the home inevitably gives rise to dependency and monotonous living. Purposeful activity beyond the confines of an institution is what serves the survival of the self."

At rare moments, he witnessed some of his patients carry out movements under hypnosis that were virtually impossible to perform without. This was the turning point in his career. Thus began a lifelong dedication, where science and religion combined, enabled and encouraged Cathal to help those less fortunate than himself.

On completing his studies, he took up a post at the Royal Hospital in Donnybrook, Dublin. There he was encouraged by the positive effects of self-hypnosis in the treatment of pain, using relaxation and imagery techniques daily with his elderly patients.

"Bringing relief to someone in pain is a blessing you cannot take for granted."

Some of his patients were over the one hundred years of age mark. This gave him a unique opportunity to listen to their deepest thoughts, experiences, memories, and dreams, allowing him greater access and insight into the workings of the mind.

"If you want to learn about life, talk to someone who has lived theirs. We can learn so much from our elderly citizens. Our duty of care is to them. By taking care of the older ones, we take care of ourselves."

Since his time at the Royal, Cathal has dedicated his life to helping others to help themselves. He runs two clinical hypnotherapy practices in Dublin, whose success is largely based on his popular website *www.hypnosis.ie*. He regularly gives lectures and radio discussions on matters concerning mental health, covering a wide range of issues within the alternative and complementary medicine fields.

Cathal believes that most symptoms can be relieved by working directly with the subconscious under the right professional guidance. He aims to help his analysands get better without holding out the promise of a cure.

"I tend to avoid giving advice, or recommending ways to live, for that is imposing and counter-productive. In therapy, my goal is to decipher the unconscious. They must know the truth, face the truth, and deal with it by making it conscious. Because repression requires a continuous expenditure of energy, my focus is on redirecting this mental energy towards newly desired goals."

Cathal makes no secret of the fact that his work to date would not have been achieved without first undertaking a thorough self-analysis. At thirty-five years of age, his direction is guided by an understanding of his vocation; it is one that is based on life experience and contact with people.

Acknowledgements

Many people have played a part in making this book happen. I would especially like to thank Roy Hunter, for his insight, experience, humanity, and enduring patience. Without his encouragement and careful editing, this book would never have been offered for publication. To Joseph Keaney, President of the Institute of Clinical Hypnotherapy and Psychotherapy (Ireland), I extend my warmest thanks for introducing me to hypnoanalysis in its purest form. My appreciation goes to Sarah O'Neill and Finbarr Moloney for their wonderful grasp of language. Thanks also to Shauna Busto Gilligan for her skillful proofreading, editing, and friendship. To my brother Dara, for his guidance and protection, to my son Fionn for his motivating smile, and to my family and friends without whose untiring faith I would not have found my vocation. Above all, I wish to acknowledge the passionate love, encouragment, and invaluable assistance my wife Amanda has given me in seeing this book through to fruition.

Cathal O'Briain, 2009

A Word from Dr. Joseph E. Keaney

Aristotle wrote:
"Before you heal the body you must first heal the mind."

It is always exciting to read *hypno-psychotherapy* works by graduate members of the Institute of Clinical Hypnotherapy and Psychotherapy, for their profession is unique in the world of hypnosis today. My deepest hope is that the knowledge set out in this book will inspire all those who need to help or better themselves, while also providing valuable assistance to others in the healing, medical, and psychological professions. The focus of *self-therapy* in this book derives partly from Cathal's intuitive understanding of the *B Chaps* model (Brief Clinical Hypnoanalytical Solution Focused Psychotherapy) and he has certainly brought a new dimension and insight to this transforming approach while simultaneously being true to the underlying concepts. I have worked closely with him in perfecting this therapeutic model, so that its rapid and effective use may continue to be used for producing lasting results within the clinical setting.

I wholeheartedly recommend this book to all those who wish to use hypnosis to bring about lasting change. It is an excellent contribution to the historical development of hypnotherapy and its concepts are soundly based on insightful methodology. If applied, they have the potency to transform your mind, body, and spirit. Set yourself free from the bondage of emotional difficulty and relish this mind expanding journey you're about to undertake. This book will literally change the way you think, feel, and behave, forever!

"It's not the conscious mind that I'm interested in. It's the unconscious mind that will make all the changes."

Dr. Joseph E. Keaney - President of the Institute of Clinical Hypnotherapy & Psychotherapy (Ireland)

Follow your heart, your mind, your desire. By that I mean follow your own heart, your own mind, your own desire.

Cathal O'Briain

Introduction

Wouldn't it be nice to be able to conquer fears, phobias, inhibitions, stress, worry and do it all by yourself. Maybe you want to quit smoking or shed a few pounds, put an end to insomnia or combat allergies and headaches. Perhaps you would like to rid your mind of compulsive traits and negative behaviors, to overcome travel fright or increase self-esteem. By reading this book you will learn how to harness the power of your subconscious mind. As a result you will have greater confidence in your ability to tackle problems that have psychological origins. I will teach you how to program your subconscious to foster health, wealth, happiness and success. As a result you'll feel great and find that goals can be easily achieved once the obstacles on your path to inner freedom have been removed.

This book will help you to overcome problems rather than endure them. No one should have to remain prisoner to their own thoughts, especially when inner-peace can be achieved through simple *mind-strengthening techniques* involving emotional control. Only by first understanding the nature of a problem and how it has been created, can you write a new behavioral pattern to override the current one that's no longer required. The conscious part of the mind doesn't know exactly what is causing your present conditions or how they can be rectified, but the subconscious knows why they exist and how they can be resolved. For it is in the subconscious that they are created in the first place.

People nowadays want to know how they can improve their lot, increase their happiness and success, and look after their health using holistic approaches involving self-understanding. The realization that many symptoms are created and maintained in the subconscious mind has grown in recent years, and *self-therapy* is increasingly being recommended as the complementary medicine of the future. What makes self-hypnosis such a desirable alternative is that healing is set at your own pace. You decide what you want and how soon you want it.

This book will teach you how to become your own therapist by laying out, in simple language, techniques and strategies for reprogramming your subconscious. Within a matter of weeks you will see life from a new perspective as changes start occurring at a deep level. You will stop looking to the future for potential happiness and begin enjoying life in the present, savoring each moment as each day is filled with new challenges.

Mind and body can work in harmony, providing you first change your negative subconscious attitudes. Exploration of the subconscious is the key to changing these attitudes, traits and beliefs that somehow become cemented in the mind over time. Self-hypnosis explores, investigates and corrects the internal language and emotion that drives behavior, while at the same time providing you with a means of quality time-out from the busy commotion of everyday living.

Anxiety laden illnesses and depression are far more commonplace now. Because people have grown more open to complementary medicine in recent years, hypnotherapy is steadily rising to the fore as one of the most powerful healing tools, bringing with it fresh new ideas and ways to tackle psychological problems. Hypnosis helps people to help themselves. By learning how to limit mental constraints in a gentle and relaxing manner, therapeutic intervention can now be conducted deep inside the subconscious, where the root of many problems originates.

If you are to make use of your deeper mind, you must first learn to harness its power. Through hypnosis the subconscious can be influenced to bring about desired change. Other similar complementary therapies such as *yoga* and *meditation* also make use of the *trance state*, bringing the user gradually into the subconscious domain, where clarity of thought is felt at a level that increases every time it's induced. In trance, the speed of your psychological reality slows down to a rate where it is understood and familiar once again. A higher, yet wholly dissimilar, state from normal conscious thought can be manifested within a short period of time, and patience is a much valued commodity when teaching yourself how to fully relax.

It is amazing the number of people who spend several hours a day watching depressing television programs, yet don't allow themselves just fifteen minutes for proper relaxation. These are the same people who can't understand why they are stressed out. Is it any wonder, considering their dedication to these programs that are somehow meant to portray real life? Self-hypnosis cuts out the noise and commotion of everyday hustle and bustle. This is when the person is usually most productive in shaping reality to suit their needs. It is a detachment from that which is material and misrepresented, and if you seek truth, balance and harmony in your life, you must accept that your journey is no longer moving outward, but rather inward.

The human mind is like an iceberg in the sea. The *conscious* is only the tip of the iceberg, that part of the *psyche* which is visible and understandable because you can inspect it. The *subconscious* is the area of your mind lying underwater, but whose volume makes up the greater part of the whole. Many difficulties, habits, compulsions, nervous disorders, neuroses and mentally generated illnesses involve some part of the subconscious. It's hard sometimes to digest the fact that the very area that is causing your problem is the same area that protects you from harm and danger every day. But this is why you must teach your subconscious to work with you instead of against you. Looking inwards through self-hypnosis is the best means of under-standing the subconscious motives behind the maintenance of a symptom.

Over the course of this book you will learn how to breathe correctly. When you have mastered correct breathing, this will give you an edge over others who do not use their breath properly in hypnosis. With many books on self-hypnosis, breathing correctly is something many therapists fail to address properly. In doing so, they possibly overlook one of the most crucial components in the self-hypnotic procedure. Correct breathing will become second nature to you, as will the implanting of suggestion and image, the other two principal factors in the self-hypnotic process.

The language, methods and techniques contained in this book are laid out clearly and are easy to remember. You will learn several self-hypnotic inductions to be practiced, and you will know which ones work best for you. Soon you will be able to achieve a deep level of trance, and with little effort. Be patient at the start and learn as much as you can about the particular area you wish to improve. It is all well and good suggesting away problems that are bothering you. But in order for real change to happen, you must first understand the source of your problem, and these two concerns: *why it has originated, and how best to overcome it.* Gaining insight into why you behave a certain way is the key to success in self-therapy, so read the entire book even if you think some of the topics I discuss do not relate to you. In due course, your subconscious will reveal the source of the problem; and when it does, you will know intuitively how best to change it.

Too much time is wasted in the battle with unrealistic fear, and too little time is invested in the sunlight with which you've been blessed. All of us want to be able to look back on our lives knowing that we've truly lived. With each tender hour that passes, the next one should be more precious than the last. The lessons have been learned, the sentences have been served and now it is time to embrace mental freedom through an opening of consciousness.

Good luck!

Part 1

Making the Most of Your Mind

"Your mind, a busy computer, carrying out the functions of the day. Its virus is negative language. Its anti-virus is positive language, or no language at all."
Cathal O'Briain

Chapter 1

Understanding Hypnosis and Self-Hypnosis

"All hypnosis is self-hypnosis."
Charles Tebbetts, 1983

What You Will Learn From This Book

Your life is about to change, and for the better. My promise to you is that by the time you have reached the end of this book, your thoughts, feelings and behaviors will have undergone a complete transformation. I will teach you how to reach deep into your subconscious mind and utilize your existing skills and resources. Restoration of control by returning your mind to *homeostasis* and *equilibrium* is the ultimate goal.

You are blessed with a wonderful mind, but there is a good chance that you may be only using a fraction of its potential. There is a reason why your subconscious has attracted you to this book. Perhaps it has fallen into your lap so that you may truly realize the power inside you. The force that you are about to bring to fruition is deep within your subconscious. Through self-hypnosis you are going to learn how to harness its power, so that you can live a more relaxed and happier life. Starting right now, let this inward journey draw an end to fear and negativity, and allow your thoughts instead to become focused on inner freedom, peace, happiness and success.

This user-friendly book is written to help you look after your mental and physical wellbeing, and to help you embrace harmonious living and good health. Each chapter provides insight into what you must do to create the sort of life you desire. But first you must accept that *change* is imminent. With the true acceptance that change is good and not something to be feared, there comes a shift in *subconscious attitude*. By changing your subconscious attitude, you begin paving the way for a happy and fulfilled life.

Hypnotic relaxation is a personal subjective experience that helps you develop intelligence, faster reflexes, and overall physical and mental well-being. Setting aside some time each day to relax must become a priority. Learning to relax helps you to overcome sabotaging behavior with its setbacks. In an altered state of mind little attention is given to the conscious, judgmental voice that often creates conflict in the first place. As we learn to switch off our critical inner voice in hypnosis, we can also learn to quieten down the outer voice that can sometimes get the better of us in the waking state. This allows us to think more clearly throughout the day instead of wasting valuable time battling with our thoughts, feelings and behaviors, which are ultimately decided by the manner in which we speak to ourselves internally.

This guide to self-hypnosis examines all the essential ingredients needed for mastering self-hypnotic trance, and gives you word for word self-hypnotic scripts that cover more than twenty different problem areas. By using these scripts, you will be able to record your very own *personalized therapy sessions*. Once you make a recording, you have it for life. You can reuse, modify or edit these recordings as suits your purposes, depending of course on the type of recording equipment you have. Whether you use an old tape recorder or the latest technology to record your voice, the hypnotic scripts contained in this book are easy to read and most effective when implanted in the subconscious. By using your own voice to implant suggestions into your mind, the self-hypnotic process is considerably bolstered. You are basically guiding your own mind into the hypnotic state. The more you do it, the easier it becomes.

Imagine for me now that you are on holidays. Involve all your senses and just feel the heat of the sun for a moment. Smell the air and listen to the sounds around you. Now I want you to bring up all the feelings and sensations that you normally associate with being on holidays. This nice, warm, relaxed feeling that you are presently experiencing in your body has being created by you, through the use of your imagination. This book will teach you how to feel this good and how to use your mind to shape your desired reality.

This book covers many aspects of the hypnotherapeutic process with a wide variety of mind-strengthening techniques. From quitting smoking to eliminating allergies, all can be achieved and with lasting results. Special attention is given to the treatment of *emotional problems* and the subject of *repression*. You will also grasp a concise and informative overview of how the mind works and a general understanding of the various emotional disorders. Consciously you will learn and subconsciously you will grow.

Only good can come from learning self-hypnosis as it is a natural, healing therapy. I have done my utmost to ensure that you learn self-hypnosis as a *pure* and *simple form*. By introducing you to basic skills that will soon become habitual, the essence of what you are about to learn is understood from the beginning. The experienced athlete draws on the most basic elements of their sport in practice sessions, as well as the latest techniques on the market to improve their game. *Trying too hard often produces less,* which is why I have constructed this book in such a way that you will learn to crawl before you can walk. Self-hypnosis is about allowing the process to happen.

I will show you how to tap into your higher-self, by giving you the necessary tools for maximum living, spiritually and psychologically. You will notice family and friends responding differently to you as you respond differently to them. You will be more in tune with yourself and better able to interact and identify with people through empathy. Concentration and memory will improve dramatically and so too will your ability to control impulse problems, habits and addictions.

Take each chapter slowly, especially the chapter on the breath, because if you do not learn to breathe correctly, self-hypnosis can become limited. Becoming your own therapist calls for patience, but the beneficial factors you gain make learning it worth the effort.

"Hypnosis is the gateway to the subconscious."
Dr. Joseph E. Keaney

What is Hypnosis?

Hypnosis is a non-addictive power for good and is a natural manifestation of the mind at work. It results in a state of consciousness dissimilar to sleep or wakefulness, where attention is drawn from the external environment and is concentrated on mental, sensory and physiological experiences. While in an *altered state*, you have the ability to change *perceptions* and *cognitions*.

At times throughout history, scientists have argued about whether or not the state of hypnotic trance actually exists. Some believe it is simply the product of *suggestion* and *expectancy* alone, and others believe it is more biological in nature, where the body becomes self-regulating in a state of heightened awareness that is not achievable in normal conscious thinking. Even today experts still differ on the exact definition of hypnosis. World renowned hypnotherapist Charles Tebbetts said that all hypnosis is self-hypnosis. Roy Hunter, who studied under Tebbetts, also considers hypnosis to be *guided daydreaming*.

One certain thing is that hypnosis produces an extraordinarily relaxed state of mind generally created through focused attention, suggestion, imagery and lack of critical conscious thought. Although we know it is very different to sleep, it still has properties that access the *REM* (rapid eye movement) state. All hypnotic phenomena involve some properties of REM which is another natural manifestation of the brain's capacity to program itself.

The subconscious is the center where mental and physical self-healing generates, and because the mind and body do not work in isolation, it is through *healing your mind* that you *heal your body*. This is why hypnosis works, and is why I define it as: *a state of relaxation, concentration and heightened awareness induced by suggestion and imagination.*

Hypnosis within the modern therapeutic context has rapidly become a popular means of freeing up the mind and body of treatable *psychosomatic disorders* (i.e. disorders that have a considerable psychological component), ranging from simpler conditions like *irritable bowel syndrome* and *insomnia* to the more complex, like *depression* and *post-traumatic stress disorder*. The word hypnosis, which derives from the Greek verb *hypnos*, meaning to sleep, was coined by the Scottish surgeon James Braid during the nineteenth century. Whatever hypnosis is, it is not sleep. It is more a form of *nervous sleep* and is increasingly being used throughout the world in addressing a wide range of physical and mental disorders. Hypnotic intervention can be an effective tool in addressing suffering and in facilitating the restoration of a sense of control. Once control has been fully restored, self-mastery is attained both psychologically and physically.

What is Self-Hypnosis?

Hetero-hypnosis is when another person, such as a hypnotherapist, induces the hypnotic state in you. Self-hypnosis is for those who wish to induce the hypnotic state in their own mind and body, and through personal, subjective means. At the most basic level, it can be viewed as an easy way to switch off for a while. But self-hypnosis is far more than just a means of relaxing the mind and body. It is an extremely effective therapeutic tool and is more commonly used in bringing about positive, desired mental and physical changes with rapid and lasting results.

Self-hypnosis helps you to help yourself, and is a powerful way to take charge of your life. It gives you the ability to be in full control, and by regaining control, you can then decide with clarity which direction you want your life to go in. Practitioners experienced in the art of self-hypnosis can hypnotize themselves with great ease and within a matter of moments.

Self-hypnosis gets us in touch with ourselves in a way that is uniquely introspective. The stillness and calmness that is felt silences the natter of conscious thinking, and brings us ever closer to what we define as the *true self*. It is in the *true self* that we encounter understanding, for the subconscious mind is the *core* of our being, and the fountain of knowledge. Without positive introspection the subconscious is left in control of us, and can only do its best to make sense of the information we pass down to it. But by using self-hypnosis as a way of living, we become its master, and it becomes our servant. This means that the information given to it now is under tight word and imagery restrictions, where unsupervised negative suggestion and imagery are no longer being passed down to it on a daily basis.

Over time as your skill increases so too does your quality of life. Problems that once seemed like they couldn't be overcome will start losing their gravity in the light of true understanding. We all have problems. How we deal with our problems is the measure of our worth. By tapping into your subconscious regularly, words like *problem* and *difficult* will have no place in your dictionary. They will be replaced with words like *solution* and *easy*. Self-hypnosis abides by strict language and imagery principles, and the subconscious only works against us when given ambiguous instructions of a negative nature. So if we are to achieve positive results, we must first understand that our deeper mind is like a very busy individual, and this individual is more than willing to help us, but only on condition that we stick to the rules of the mind.

Self-hypnosis is a way of breaking free of old habits the mind gets into over the years, and by moving out of the comfort zone of ritualistic behavior, the chains of negative self-preoccupation are broken. What stops us moving forward with courage is an unrealistic fear that change could spell danger. But self-hypnosis removes this fear by encouraging change to happen subtly instead of dramatically. Soon you find yourself doing the things you once feared you could not. This is because you have allowed your mind to experience change in a natural progression, instead of expecting positive results to happen by jumping in the deep end with a feeling of uncertainty. Self-hypnosis helps you decide what you want and when you want it.

Through self-therapy we can overcome even the most difficult of disorders. By harnessing the power of our subconscious we learn that the answers to various problems and symptoms lie not in our external environment, but rather are found within the capacity of our mind and belief system. My goal is to give you the necessary tools for living life to the full, by first getting you back to basics concerning the mechanisms of the mind and the way in which you use it. The human mind is very complex biologically, but the way to master it psychologically is rather basic. If you stick to the rules that are laid out in this book, within a short space of time a profound change will start taking place; and this change will bring you success, empowerment, and inner freedom.

The Hypnotic Induction

Hypnosis begins with a *hypnotic induction*. Breath, suggestion, misdirected attention and imagery all play their part in directing your mind towards achieving total relaxation. The induction helps you to become absorbed through heightened inner experience, positive feelings, clearer perceptions, and enhanced thought processes.

The Hypnotic Formula

Hypnosis can be understood and described by the following formula:

Misdirected attention + imagination + belief + expectation = hypnosis

Little is required to achieve the hypnotic state and this explains why we drift in and out of trance so easily and regularly each day. Because the subconscious primarily influences behavior, by tapping into its power you automatically start using the larger portion of your mind, thus initiating more control over behavior and impulse response. Hypnotic susceptibility depends largely on motivation and lack of skepticism, so having an open-minded and enthusiastic approach to self-hypnosis will significantly help the process of self-change to manifest itself more quickly.

Is Hypnosis Similar to Daydreaming?

Yes. It is very similar indeed as both involve the same brainwave activity known as *alpha waves*. In fact, as I mentioned earlier, author Roy Hunter considers hypnosis to be *guided daydreaming*. Lying on a bed or simply relaxing on an armchair is a good way to induce a trance, but a trance is something that can be created anywhere and at any time. All you have to do is let your mind wander off into a pleasant daydream where it can roam freely without the interference of conscious thought. The reason you slip naturally in and out of hypnotic daydreams is because at certain times of the day your conscious mind likes to switch off for a while; and when your conscious mind takes a nap like this, the subconscious then comes to the fore to protect us. It acts as a *third eye* and safeguards us from any presenting dangers that could arise while we are not giving the external environment our full attention.

Daydreaming is a brain activity that occurs quite a lot throughout the day and is largely an unconscious one. We are all naturally-skilled participants in this *time-out* therapy and the increased level of concentration we achieve in trance automatically promotes relaxation, clarity of thought and stimulation of positive image. How often have you found yourself staring at an object intensely while your mind just wanders and sifts through memories, images, events and future premonitions? It's as if our mind is having a stretch before getting back to the busy mode of thinking. All too often it happens when someone is boring you to tears in conversation; the mind just wanders away while you narrow your attention to the spot on their chin, imagining what it must be like to live alone on a desert island. It's typically done when you are bored or tired, but is something you shouldn't just keep reserved for when you need a break from your external environment. Self-hypnosis takes full advantage of this natural manifestation.

Should I be Concerned About Using Hypnosis?

No. Hypnosis is a proven therapeutic aid that has been practiced formally for centuries, but in reality has been used for thousands of years. Each and every day of our lives we naturally slip in and out of the hypnotic state.

Are Drugs Ever Used?

They are not necessary. Hypnosis is completely natural. It must never be used in conjunction with drugs unless your personal physician advises it for some very rare and unusual circumstance. This would be acting in direct opposition to the principles that govern the safe and ethical use of hypnosis. If you are currently on medication for a particular mental or physical problem, please continue to take it. Self-hypnosis is safe to use while on certain prescribed drugs, but only with your doctor's permission. As for any other types of addictive or illegal drug, these are absolutely out of the question.

Am I Asleep During Hypnosis?

Your mind is aware, but you are extremely relaxed, almost on the brink of sleep. Hypnosis alters perception and awareness in a way that is quite different from normal sleep. This natural and healthy ability to induce trance is manifested through basic relaxation, and has been in practice since the dawn of time.

In the next chapter, I will be discussing the origins and evolution of hypnosis, from early man to the present day. Self-hypnosis should be understood as a pure and natural form of *self-healing*, as its reputation today has been cleansed and purified by the valiant work of the pioneers that have gone before us.

Chapter 2

Insight into an Age-Old Tradition

"Hypnosis is a product of evolution. Generated naturally, and through necessity, the subconscious has risen to the fore to protect, heal and to calm the mind."
Cathal O'Briain

The Myths and Misconceptions about Hypnosis

The hypnosis profession struggles with a tarnished reputation in the medical field as well as in other areas of therapy. Many stage hypnotists are partly responsible for misrepresenting hypnosis and promoting a negative image but Hollywood also shares the blame. A number of *b-grade* movies misrepresent hypnosis, promoting the idea that hypnosis is about *mind control* rather than *mind strengthening*. This chapter discusses some of the common myths and misconceptions created by this misrepresentation.

Myth No. 1: I Lose Control of my Will (Svengali Effect)

This myth evolved as a result of negative exposure, for example, stage shows, television films, books and so on. The work of the stage hypnotist is largely the result of a very careful selection of subjects and the expectancies of these subjects while on stage or in the audience. The hypnotist will only pick those who are ready to think, imagine and comply with his or her requests and demands. In real hypnosis nobody can be made to do something against their *will*. If a suggestion was to be given in hypnosis that went against the *belief system* of an individual, they would automatically awaken from the hypnotic state. The idea that a person's *will* can be controlled is known as the *Senegal Effect*, and gained its name from an old John Barry more film called *Senegal*. In this film a deranged old man hypnotizes women to go out and commit crimes under his spell. It's a good example of how misconceptions can develop over time through unhelpful exposure to films like this. The truth is the subconscious will ignore a command if it is not within its interest. A hypnotized person will automatically arouse into normal wakefulness if they are being asked to do something that goes against their will. Hypnotherapist Roy Hunter once bounced out of deep hypnosis simply because the hypnotist asked him to shave off his beard.

Myth No. 2: A Person is Unconscious while in the Hypnotic State

In hypnosis you are fully aware and even more receptive than normal. The *five senses* are also at an increased level of receptivity, so should an emergency arise, you can open your eyes and automatically come out of trance. There is never a loss of consciousness while in hypnosis, no matter how deep into trance you go.

Myth No. 3: A Person may get Stuck in Hypnosis

This is completely false. There has never been a recorded case of anyone *getting stuck* in the hypnotic state. Hypnosis is a pleasant state of relaxation which one can be easily aroused from. However, if your body required natural sleep, you could go from hypnosis into a comfortable sleep state if not awakened by the hypnotherapist. You would awaken later, just as you would after a nap (or a full night's sleep).

Myth No. 4: Only the Weak-Minded can be Hypnotized

False. Self-hypnosis requires a level of understanding and intelligence. Anyone who desires to hypnotize themselves can do so, but the level of trance we achieve depends largely on our skill and intuition. A gentleman once said to me, "You won't be able to hypnotize me."

To which I replied, "Yes, you're right, I won't."

The late Charles Tebbetts taught that people can resist hypnosis if they want to.

The Underlying Principle

The use of hypnosis establishes a climate for healing because it creates a relaxed atmosphere. In this relaxed atmosphere there is an increase in motivation and energy because you are the active participant in your own positive, mental and physical treatment. Hypnosis can raise the pain threshold and provide one with an opportunity for self-mastery. Within each and every one of us are the necessary resources for personal development, but change must happen at an unconscious level first before we can create new behavioral patterns for maximum living. This is where hypnosis plays its part; it is the connection that links us to our deeper mind.

Hypnosis: A Brief History

In reality, hypnosis originated at the dawn of human civilization. Even early man had the ability to daydream and wonder, naturally projecting images of the hunt and procreation into reality; his objectives uninhibited by logic and driven purely by instinct. The simplicity which once beset the evolving mind created the perfect mental environment for self-hypnosis to work. Little has changed over forty-two thousand years, except perhaps that now we measure and study ourselves more consciously, even if this means going against the grain and natural progression of hypnosis.

Modern hypnosis is roughly two hundred years old but has been around since ancient times under different names and used in a wide variety of cultures, by their priests, shamans, healers, and medicine men. The first person to attempt integrating hypnosis into modern medicine was a charasmatic viennese physician called Franz Anton Mesmer (1734–1815). Mesmer, who gave his name to *mesmerism,* believed that the human body had magnetic polarity and he termed this universal force animal *magnetism.*

"Mesmers theory of animal magnetism was a mishmash of astrological and physiological ideas derived largely from the work of Paracelsus (1493-1541) some two hundred earlier (Goldsmith, 1934)."

"Paracelsus assumed that magnets were responsible for curing disease (Goldberg, 2005)."

Mesmer believed that the human body responded to gravitational forces caused by moving planets in the universe, and that disease is caused by a disruption in this gravitational fluid present in all of us. Mesmer believed that he had an abundance of this gravitational fluid, which he could pass to others. He was a showman with great presence, and going through an elaborate ritual, he would direct *magnetic fluid* down an iron wand, which he would then wave at his subjects, sometimes putting his wand aside and directing the fluid with his eyes. Unfortunately his showmanship drew the attention of the French government, who after an investigation, denounced him as a fraud and a charlatan. Benjamin Franklin came from America to participate in the investigation of Mesmer's work. Frankln correctly observed that Mesmer's results were because of the power of imagination and warranted further investigation.

"But he was quickly put on a ship back to America after local scientists found a way to use Franklin's comments as further evidence to denounce Mesmer (Hunter, 2000)."

"Dr. Charles D'Elson, one of Mesmer's protégées, defended his teacher by saying:

"If Mesmer had no other secret than that he has been able to make the imagination exert an influence upon health, would he not still be a wonder doctor? If treatment by the use of the imagination is the best treatment, why do we not make use of it? (Goldsmith, 1934).""

"After enjoying considerable popularity and fame for many years, Mesmer retired to Switzerland where he died in 1815. The next chapter in the history of hypnosis is the story of one of Mesmer's very own students, whose name was the Marquis de Puysegur (1751-1825). In 1784, at the age of thirty-three years, the Marquis de Puysegur discovered how to lead a client into a deep trance state called *somnambulism* using relaxation and calming techniques. The term *somnambulism* is still widely used among hypnotherapists today in reference to a deep hypnotic trance state (Richard MacKenzie, 2006)."

"After the controversial Mesmer, the succession was direct and continuous. These English surgeons, including: John Elliotson; James Braid; and James Esdaile; were successful at using hypnosis as a surgical anaesthetic (Goldsmith, 1934)."

"Scottish-born surgeon James Braid (1796-1860) continued investigating hypnotherapeutic procedures and was responsible for changing the name *mesmerism* to *hypnotism*. Although Braid is credited with coining the term *hypnotism*, others had used this term before him (Gravitz & Gerton, 1984).""

When Braid discovered later on in his research that the hypnotic state and all its phenomena could be achieved without the subject being asleep, he then realized that he had to change the name hypnosis (which derives from the Greek verb *hypnos* meaning *to sleep*) to *monoideism* but by then it was too late, and the name hypnosis remains to this day.

Another Scottish surgeon, James Esdaile (1808-1859), while working in India, performed thousands of serious operations using hypnosis as the sole pain-killing agent. Persecuted by the authorities, Esdaile suffered a similar fate to others working in this new field, with charges of sacrilege brought against him for removing the pain that God intended us to feel.

In 1831, Dr. John Elliotson (1791-1868) was elected Professor of the Principles and Practice of Physic at London University. Like his fellow physicians who practiced mesmerism, Elliotson too suffered the wrath of the medical establishment, and so retired to investigate and practice hypnotic techniques further.

"Braid, Esdaile, and Elliotson gave hypnosis a more respectable reputation within certain medical arenas; but due to its direct links to mesmerism, hypnosis remained shunned as quackery by the medical, political and religous establishments. With the introduction of the surgical anaesthetic, hypnosis then entered a quiet period, until its revival in the 1800's by a French physician named Ambrose Auguste Liebeault (1823-1904). Liebeault, who first postulated suggestion as a mechanism behind theraputic hypnosis, started the School of Nancy which was clinical in nature (Goldsmith, 1934)."

"His integrity, selflessness, devotion to the needy, and success with hypnosis attracted the attention of Hyppolyte Bernheim (1837-1919), a renowned neurologist from Nancy, who, at first skeptical, later became an ardent proponent of hypnosis. Together they developed Braid's theories and treated over 12,000 patients (Goldberg, 2005)."

Around the same time a second and quite different school of thought emerged with the opening of the Salpetriere School, founded by Jean Martin Charcot (1835-1893), whose aim was to study hypnosis as a neurosis rather than as an actual treatment.

Charcot's discoveries on hypnosis and hysteria were presented to the French Academy of Sciences. Pierre Janet (1859-1947) a French physician, psychiatrist, and philosopher, followed on from Charcot and it was Janet who discovered the dissociation theory of hypnosis. Janet was influential in establishing a true connection between academic psychology and the clinical treatment of mental illnesses.

"It is interesting that Sigmund Freud (1856–1939), who of course is considered to be the father of modern psychology, studied hypnosis at both the Nancy and Salpetriere Schools (Freud, 1963), but then chose to abandon the use of hypnosis almost entirely. Initially, Freud tried to use hypnosis to recover traumatic memories from the unconscious (Malcolm, 1982)."

Freud wasn't particularly good at inducing the hypnotic state in his patients; and this led him to frustration on many occassions, until he eventually abandoned hypnosis and started using other methods to lift repression.

"Ultimately, he developed other ways to achieve his goal, namely to treat neurotic illness by accessing the subconscious via the analysis of transferance and the interpretation of dreams. However, Freud may not have abandoned the technique entirely (Gravitz & Gurton, 1981)."

By the end of the nineteenth century Kraft Ebing, Wetterstrand, Albert Moll and many other famous physicians were also making positive discoveries regarding the clinical use of hypnosis.

Émile Coué (1857-1926), a French psychologist and pharmacist, introduced a new method of psychotherapy based on the simple use of *auto-suggestion* or *self-suggestion*, whereby a person repeats suggestions to themselves in order to spur the imagination. He believed that where there was *conflict* between the *will* and the *imagination,* the imagination invariably wins the battle. So rather than using will power alone, one must also make use of their imagination to better health. He believed that repetition of suggestion increased the likelihood of images being projected into reality; most especially when implanted in the morning, and again before sleeping. Coue learned hypnosis from Liébeault and in 1913 founded the Lorraine Society of Applied Psychology.

By the 1920s, hypnosis was the subject of much experimental investigation by respected psychologists such as Clark L. Hull (1884-1952). But it was not until after World War II that hypnosis became popular once again in the clinical field; used mainly in the treatment of battle related disorders, *post-traumatic stress disorder* and *war neurosis.* As a result of its post-war success, it gained the endorsement of several medical authorities around the world, most notably the *British Medical Association* and the *American Medical Association.* One man responsible for its widespread recognition back then and its clinical uses in the present was the pioneer Milton Erickson.

Milton Erickson (1901-1980), who is considered to be the father of modern hypnosis, suffered with many handicaps from an early age.

"Erickson said, "Everyone is as individual as their own thumb print."

In his practice, he tailored every induction to the client's individual needs and perceptual bias. He believed in the wisdom of the unconscious mind, and in the theory that people have all the resources necessary to make changes inside themselves (O'Brien, 2004).

Dave Elman (1900-1967) was another pioneer of the medical use of hypnosis. Although Elman had received no medical training, he is known for having trained the most physicians and psychotherapists in America, in the use of hypnotism. He is also known for introducing rapid inductions to the field of hypnotism (Wikepedia).

Since that time, hypnosis has gained much recognition and acceptance by the medical fraternity as well as other therapeutic institutions, thanks to the work of pioneers such as John Grindler (gesalt therapist) and Richard Bandler (linguist), who discovered Neuro Linguistic Programming in the 1970s from the work of Milton Erickson and renowned family therapist Virginia Satir.

Also in recent history, one of the most prominent figures responsible for the evolution of hypnosis and self-hypnosis was Irishborn Dr. Jack Gibson.

"As a surgeon, Dr. Gibson carried out over four thousand procedures using hypnosis instead of anesthetic. These included major operations, surgical procedures and treatment of dislocations and fractures [...]. Jack Gibson graduated from the Royal College of Surgeons, Dublin, in 1933, having won almost every available medal (gold and silver in Anatomy and Operative Surgery) [...]. After the outbreak of war, he worked in England as a surgeon in the hospitals of the Emergency Medical Service. He treated numerous soldiers, wounded at Dunkirk during *D Day* and held the most senior surgical post in Ethiopia.

Back in Ireland, he took up the post of County Surgeon in Naas, Co. Kildare and continued to develop his method of deep relaxation as an alternative to anesthesia and drugs and devoted himself to using hypnosis as a mind-strengthening, relaxation therapy, to overcome any mental or physical condition (Dr Jack Gibson, 2004)."

Hypnosis has had its ups and downs throughout history; but thanks to the work of pioneering men such as Jack Gibson and the above mentioned, men who often faced ridicule and sometimes even ruin, hypnosis still continues to be popularly used in the control and relief of many of today's mental and physical problems. The results speak for themselves, and they are well documented and backed up with scientific proof and evidence.

"Another man worth mentioning is Charles Tebbetts, who earned the title of a *grandmaster teacher* of hypnosis from Dr. John Hugues, a major researcher for an American hypnosis association. Tebbetts, who became legendary for teaching client centered hypnotism, started his hypnosis career in 1927 as a stage hypnotist. Initially, the young Tebbetts devoted himself to the entertainment side of hypnosis. After many months, a doctor (who was a friend of the family) saw him perform one night in Beatrice, Nebraska, his mother's hometown. The physician persuaded the young hypnotist to work with him and with his patients. After considerable experiments, the doctor learned the art of hypnosis himself; but skepticism among his peers caused the physician to swear Charlie to silence, and they parted ways (Hunter, 2005)."

After his sad parting with the doctor, Tebbetts took a detour into an advertising career for many years, and he moved to Hollywood, where he met his wife and continued his hypnotic research. His most profound research was his own complete personal recovery from a totally paralyzing stroke, accomplished with self-hypnosis. In 1970 he met Gil Boyne, who persuaded him to return to hypnosis full time; then Tebbetts and his wife moved north of Seattle to establish their own Hypnotism Training Institute. Although well known for pioneering a complex hypnotic technique called parts therapy, Tebbetts firmly believed in self-hypnosis.

In 1992, while attending a national hypnosis convention,

Tebbetts suffered a heart attack and survived only a few hours. Prior to his passing, he asked Roy Hunter to continue teaching parts therapy, and to preserve his other client centered teachings. Hunter's hypnosis career originally started in 1983, studying under Charles Tebbetts. After his mentor's passing, Hunter preserved the client centered teachings of Tebbetts by writing two hypnosis texts, which are used in numerous hypnosis schools around the world. More recently he wrote a third text that is devoted to parts therapy, *Hypnosis for Inner Conflict Resolution: Introducing Parts Therapy* (2005, Crown House Publishing). Hunter teaches that the goal of the hypnotherapist should be to help clients attain their ideal empowerment, and that clients must have the opportunity to learn self-hypnosis. He also believes that science and hypnotherapy should cooperate more and conduct more research into the benefits of hypnosis, because there is a large "undiscovered country"

of the subconscious. Hunter told me, 'I believe that we are only touching the top of the tip of the iceberg of the potential of the inner mind'.

Considering we still only use a portion of our minds' potential, hypnosis is still in its infancy with regard to its potential. So long as we push our minds further, the evolution of hypnosis will continue to provide new ways to overcome age-old problems.

Questions to Ask Yourself Before Embarking on Hypnosis
Why do I want to learn self-hypnosis?
What specific areas of improvement will I use hypnosis for?
Am I willing to dedicate a half hour to it everyday?
How can I help myself and others by practicing self-hypnosis?

What You Must Do To Make Hypnosis Happen?
Want it to happen.

Expect it to happen.
Imagine it happening.
Allow it to happen.

Should I be Seeing a Professional Therapist?

There are certain psychological and emotionally induced illnesses that are best left to the qualified therapist or healthcare professional, but this doesn't mean that self-hypnosis cannot be used in conjunction with professional treatment.

Understanding Psychosomatic Illness

Psychosomatic or *psycho-physiological* illness involves the mind and body. Physical symptoms can originate emotionally or mentally and will occur where there is weakness or vulnerability in a body part due to stress. Loss of a job can exacerbate an ulcer or cause a person to lose their hair. Marital problems could mean high blood pressure for one person and irritable bowel for another. What affects one person emotionally can affect another person physically. Mental factors affect medical conditions. Sometimes these psychological factors can cause existing symptoms to worsen. If mental factors exist behind a physical condition, it's important then that both mental and physical symptoms be treated simultaneously. Surgery and medication for liver damage from alcohol abuse is of little use to someone who won't tackle the mental reasons for drinking so heavily in the first place. *Denial* is another cause of psychosomatic illness. An example would be someone going through the anxiety of losing someone close to them and repressing the idea that they are truly gone. Psychosomatic illness often goes unnoticed as well as untreated by the sufferer.

How Does Self-Hypnosis Work?

In order for you to change your behavior, you must first change your behavioral programming. Self-hypnosis allows you to change old behavioral programs into new and more positive ones. This is done through *auto-suggestion*. *Auto-suggestion* is where you implant suggestions into your subconscious using your own internal voice and language. It can be done both in and out of hypnosis. When you implant positive suggestions into your deeper mind, the old program then becomes replaced by a new and more beneficial one. As a result the new behavioral pattern now acts in accordance with the writing of the new program. The chosen program then remains until such time as the subject wishes to change it.

Through self-hypnosis you have the ability to change your behavioral pattern into the type of person you desire to be. The reason self-hypnosis works so effectively is because when you are implanting positive suggestions, there is no intrusion of conscious thinking. It is *by-passed* through breathing, concentrated attention, deepening (ability to deepen the level of trance) and auto-suggestion. Because the subconscious does not have the ability to reason, it simply accepts what it's told as truth, even if it is not true. Like a child it takes everything literally; so when you tell it you are confident and relaxed, it believes it, especially when you imagine it. This process of behavioral change comes about when you allow it to happen naturally in a relaxed state of trance; and you may then reinforce it in the waking state through *breathing with positive suggestion*, a technique you will learn in upcoming chapters.

If you are going to change your present behavioral pattern into a new one, you first need to master the art of relaxing. Relaxing is different from sleeping; and if you find it difficult to stay awake while practicing, you can suggest to yourself in the hypnotic state not to fall asleep. The time it takes you to relax may be longer in your first attempts at self-hypnosis; but before long, what took fifteen minutes will eventually only take a few seconds. As you become skilled at relaxing, you will be able to recognize a deeply relaxed state, and achieve it easily. Some people have a natural ability to let go, while others have to work harder at it. Humans are the only animals on earth who *try* to fall asleep. All other animals just allow themselves to fall asleep. Trying involves *effort*, and effort is a *conscious process* that only tends to keep you awake. If you want to fall asleep you must first relax the mind and body and then allow it to happen naturally. The same goes for self-hypnosis. You must not *try* to move into the hypnotic state; rather you should simply *allow* it to happen, as hypnosis is a natural manifestation of the mind. Hypnosis happens all by itself; and by relaxing the mind and body completely through the breath, you can move into a trance state easily and naturally. The main thing is to take your time and use your breath well. A brand new program is in the making, so relax and enjoy making it.

What does Self-Hypnosis Help With?

Hypnosis can help with the following: *addictions, agoraphobia, allergies, anger, anxiety, arthritis, asthma, assertiveness, bed-wetting, behavioral change, bereavement, blood pressure, blushing, cancer, claustrophobia, compulsions, confidence, control, dental preparation, depression, driving-test preparation, eating disorders, emotional problems, energy enhancement, exam nerves, eye contact, fear, fetishes, frustration, goal-setting, guilt feelings, habit control, headaches, independence, inferiority complexes, inhibitions, inner freedom, insomnia, irritable bowel syndrome, memory recall and enhancement, menstrual tension, migraines, motivation, mood management, nail-biting, nervous tension, nightmares, pain control, panic attacks, personal development, phobias, psychological problems, procrastination, professional development, public speaking, relationship problems, restlessness, self-esteem, self-sabotage, sexual problems, shame, shyness, skin disorders, smoking cessation, sports psychology, stage fright, stress management, study, stuttering, success, surgery preparation and recovery, trauma, travel fright, twitching, ulcers, warts, weight-reduction, worry* and many other problems and symptoms where emotional or psychological forces are at work.

Note: *a number of the above may require a referral from a licensed health care professional before you see a hypnotherapist. Also, if you use self-hypnosis for a medical condition, be sure to consult with the appropriate health care professional regarding your goal and its progress.*

Self-hypnosis is useful for almost anything and is especially useful for combating stress and increasing the energy of the mind. *Self-improvement* comes about through *self-help,* and self-hypnosis is one of the easiest and safest ways to help yourself.

Chapter 3

Powerful Suggestion for a Powerful Mind

"Avoid being mastered by your mind, and instead learn how to become a Mastermind."
Ormond McGill

In this chapter, I will be discussing the *principles of suggestion* and how they influence your mind both in and out of the hypnotic state. You will also learn about the basic structure of the mind and how each component operates individually. In order for self-hypnosis to be successful, you must first learn how to phrase suggestions correctly before implanting them. When you give yourself a suggestion and put positive emotional intent behind it, the chance of it being carried out in reality significantly increases. So it's important to believe in what you are saying if you want an idea to *take root* in your deeper mind. Once a suggestion, idea or belief has been accepted, your subconscious will then do everything in its power to make your desired intention a reality.

About Suggestion

When you are in a relaxed state such as hypnosis, your subconscious is more receptive to suggestion than when in a fully conscious state. It's the simplest form of a conditioned reflex, but has the power to become a belief, modify behavior and produce an *effect* or *action*. When one suggestion after another is accepted by the subconscious, it means that more difficult suggestions can then be accepted also. This is what is known as *abstract conditioning*. *Auto-suggestion* (self-suggestion or auto-therapy) is the easiest way to communicate internally to the subconscious. In hypnosis, you are far more suggestible than in normal wakefulness. When you make use of the trance state for inducing suggestion, the conscious mind is then far less likely to interfere in the form of argument. This allows the process of implanting suggestion to be more successful than if you were simply to give your mind an instruction to change. Even in a light state of hypnosis, suggestibility is significantly increased.

When the television is on you naturally slip into a *light state of trance* as you become engrossed in what you are watching. Advertisers use this to their advantage by repeating suggestive adverts over and over again until their messages have sunk deeply into your programming. Because your concentration is so focused and absorbed, you often don't respond to questions being asked of you by others present in the room, even though at some level you can hear them. It is during this period of narrowed awareness that suggestion has the most effect, and is why television is probably the most popular medium for persuasive advertisement. *Repetition* is the key to selling an idea to your deeper mind. But if you allow yourself to get too bombarded with externally induced suggestion, this is when your mind can become confused as to what your real aspirations are.

As children we are given suggestions by our parents that are understood and believed as fact in our developing mind. The mother plays a role similar to that of a hypnotherapist. With *belief* and *expectancy* the child looks into its mother's eyes eagerly awaiting words of unconditional love and encouragement. Then the words come and are registered deeply in the uncritical subconscious. As we develop, instructions given to us in our earlier years remain subconsciously, shaping us into the product of our parents' suggestions. It is only when we start becoming influenced by the wider world that we begin to formulate the ability to make up our own minds through auto-suggestion.

Children are very impressionable. Suggestion greatly affects the way they behave and adapt to society. Consider what happens if an intelligent child is told repeatedly, "You'll never learn," or told, "You can't do anything right."

Negative suggestions like these, if repeated often enough, could greatly reduce their ability to reach full potential. This fact has been validated by many clients in hypnotherapy offices over the years.

Suggestion is received and acted upon whether of a positive or negative nature. This explains why you can go from being in good to bad form, or from feeling healthy to feeling sick. On meeting someone you could be asked, "Are you ok? You look a little under the weather." Even though you feel perfectly fine, this could give rise to a change in mood and physical well-being, if you were to believe them. Twenty minutes later someone else could say, "You don't seem yourself today."

At this stage you might respond by saying, "There's nothing wrong with me, I'm fine!"

By now their negative suggestions could have already sunk deeply and turned you into the exact opposite of how you felt originally. This is how easily suggestion can affect you, for it is at the center of why you think, feel and act in the manner you do. It is one of the most common causes of emotional disturbance. This is why you must be on your guard from negative suggestion at all times.

> *"Suggestion is the fuel that powers the Psyche."*
> **Cathal O'Briain**

Using Suggestion Wisely

Almost every second of the day you communicate to your subconscious through suggestion. How you use suggestion is under your control. So if you want your outlook on life to be positive, you must phrase suggestions positively. The subconscious acts upon your internal language believing that the information you are giving it is true. So it's important that from this moment on, you remove any negative suggestions that you may have in your dictionary at present. This is done by giving your mind positively phrased suggestions on a regular basis in the form of repeated affirmations, both in self-hypnosis and throughout the day.

One way of combating negative suggestion is by not being too hard on yourself whenever you make a mistake or slip up. Making mistakes is part of being human. But being hard on yourself with language, such as *I'm an idiot*, only serves to help you make the same mistakes again. Whenever you call yourself a name like *idiot* the subconscious acts in accordance with your belief system. Then it goes about doing everything in its power to fulfill what it believes is your desired intention. The reason why some people develop anxiety and depression is because at some stage they may have begun reinforcing a suggestion that was made by someone else, a suggestion such as, "I think you may be suffering from depression."

This suggestion may have come from a reputable source in a time of emotional need. As a result it may have been believed, implanted and reinforced from that point on. This is why you must have your earmuffs on in the presence of potentially life changing words.

When you shape suggestions correctly through positive affirmation you are defining how you want your character and reality to be. By remaining vigilant with the language you use, there is less chance of falling victim to that which you fear becoming. Understanding that your mind is highly susceptible to suggestive influence puts you in a better position to recognize words that could potentially have a negative or even detrimental effect upon you. So whenever you hear a suggestion like *life is tough*, the way you stop these words having a negative effect upon you is by replacing them immediately with the suggestion *life is good*.

In this chapter you will learn the *principal laws* governing the use of suggestion. This will give you a clear understanding of how to carefully monitor the internal language of your mind. The most important concept to remember regarding suggestion is: *imagination is the language of the subconscious*. This means that the wording must indicate the desired result rather than focusing on the problem. In other words, keep the affirmation positive rather than negative. For example, *I am confident* is better than *I am not afraid*.

If you have not used positive affirmations before, like *I am happy,* or *I feel great*, it may seem a little strange at the beginning and may feel as though you are lying to yourself. Whether you feel happy or not, the suggestion *I am happy* is believed and accepted by the subconscious as fact, especially if there is *belief* and *expectancy* put behind it. If this type of suggestion is reinforced through repetition, within a short period of time your deeper mind will accept that this is your desired intention and will go about making the necessary changes to make real your suggestion. One does not have to be in trance for suggestion to take effect. But the reason we apply suggestion in the hypnotic state is so there is little or no opposition made by the conscious mind which has now been by-passed through concentration and relaxation.

When receiving suggestions the subconscious has the IQ of an intelligent child, so avoid using long words or complicated phrases. Simple, positive and direct words have the greatest effect, so keep it basic! Make sure the suggestions you give yourself are not beyond your capabilities. Suggestions must coincide with your belief system and be achievable in reality. *Repetition* is what reinforces suggestion and helps make it become an instinctive part of your behavioral program. The more you repeat a suggestion, the deeper it *takes root*. For this reason we must choose our words wisely. Use words like *I am* instead of *I will*. If you give the subconscious a suggestion to be carried out at some vague point in the future, there's a good chance that when you get to the day in question, it will have forgotten what you asked of it. Keep suggestions in the present tense and say them as if they are an already accomplished fact. The same goes for commands to be carried out in the future, for example, "It's June the 10th, the day of my speech. I am confident and relaxed, and I am delivering an excellent speech to all assembled."

If the mind is told *I am confident*, it registers this suggestion as something that is already true and accomplished, and not as something that is vague and distant like *I will be confident*. Here are some examples of present tense suggestions:

Present Tense
I am
It is
I feel

Future Tense
I will
It will
I will feel

When implanting suggestions or important goals you wish to achieve, make sure to work on one goal at a time. If you give your subconscious too many goals at once, it only gets confused. For example, if you want to give up smoking, stay focused on that goal and don't overload your mind with a list of other things you want to give up as well. It's best to deal with one area of improvement at a time.

Keep all suggestions focused positively on the desired result and avoid using negative suggestions. This is called the law of reversed effect. People often give themselves negative suggestions even when their intentions are good, for example, "I won't eat chocolate cake or sweets."

This type of suggestion only spurs the imagination to render an image of chocolate cake and sweets. Once this image has taken root in the subconscious, it must be carried out in reality. What the mind perceives, the mind achieves. So what you should be saying is "I enjoy eating healthy food," instead of "I won't eat chocolate cake or sweets."

Now a picture of healthy food is being imagined in the mind and the subconscious can clearly understand what foods are desirable for you to eat. I'll have more to say about the law of reversed effect in the next chapter.

Remember to keep the most important suggestions till last. The subconscious remembers all suggestions it is given, but it can more readily carry out ones given towards the end of the self-hypnotic session. Make sure to use words that have emotion and feeling behind them such as wonderful, great, beautiful, powerful, successful, proud, etc. When you say them in your mind, say them with conviction.

The Three Psychological Laws of Suggestion

At the heart of hypnosis is suggestion and central to suggestion are three laws:

> The law of reversed effect
> The law of concentrated attention
> The law of dominant effect

The Law of Reversed Effect

Because we hate what we fear, we invest it with great energy. The subconscious, like a computer has no power over itself nor has it the ability to reason. So, if an idea does take root in the subconscious, then that idea must be discharged in the motor action and regrettably, this holds true for good ideas as well as bad.

Emile Coue (French Pharmacist) believed that where there is conflict between the *imagination* and the *conscious will*, the imagination will always win the day. When the will attempts to oppose or to command the imagination, *the law of reversed effect* applies and the will's efforts are reversed into the exact opposite. For example, ask a person to walk across a plank of wood on the ground and they should be able to do so quite easily. Ask the same person to imagine that the plank is now a thousand feet up, going from one building to another. Now their reaction is very different. Often they will extend their arms in an effort to balance themselves. This is on account of their imagination commanding their will. Most people would imagine falling off, which would actually increase their risk of falling!

The Law of Concentrated Attention

When people concentrate their attention upon an idea, that idea, according to the law of concentrated attention, tends to become realized.

The Law of Dominant Effect

This principle states that a *strong emotion* tends to replace a *weaker one*. If a strong emotion is attached to a suggestion it is more likely that the suggestion will be effective.

Suggestion and Conditioned Reflexes

A *conditioned reflex* is a reflex response to a stimulus established by training. When you react to an external stimulus that bears no relationship to your current behavior but is associated to it in some way, this is a conditioned reflex. Often people try to figure out why they have behaved a certain way in a given situation, but the answer to why they behaved that way is likely to be connected to a past experience where they responded in a similar way to a similar stimulus. Reflexes work both ways. What can become a habit response can also become a skilled response. If conditioning works in the wrong way it can bring up automatic emotions of hurt, anger, guilt, hostility which give rise to detrimental reactions.

Conditioned reflexes are a major cause of emotional difficulties. Words and suggestions are often the trigger mechanism behind a reflex. And when there's emotion attached to a word, the word gains potency in the subconscious. Most conditioned reflexes are caused by responding to a non-natural external stimulus, but positive reflex actions can also be created through a conditioned response to certain emotionally implanted words which act as stimuli.

> *"Hypnotic suggestions administered at the peak of emotion*
> *are like heat seeking*
> *missiles that find their target."*
> **Dr. Joseph E. Keaney**

The Importance of Post-Hypnotic Suggestions, Cues and Symbols

Post-hypnotic suggestions are suggestions to be carried out in the future that have been implanted in the present through hypnosis. You can use a post-hypnotic suggestion to create an unconscious action or response in the waking state or in further self-hypnotic sessions. When in trance you could suggest to your subconscious that the next time you enter hypnosis, you will find yourself drifting down much quicker and deeper into relaxation. This readies the subconscious to expect and desire what you have suggested.

A good way to implant a post-hypnotic suggestion is by generating an image, color or object in your mind that stimulates the desired response.

"Whenever I induce self-hypnosis, I automatically think of a calm, blue sea. This image sends me very deep into relaxation."

In self-hypnosis an *image* is worth a thousand words. This is why imagination must play a vital role in the implantation of post-hypnotic suggestions.

Post-hypnotic cues are used to *trigger* post-hypnotic suggestions at some point after the hypnotic session. A post-hypnotic cue can be a thought, word, image, action or event that is used to create the desired response. If your goal is to feel relaxed while public speaking, you could suggest that every time you look at the audience, their faces will be a cue to slow down and feel even more relaxed. The golfer could give him or herself a post-hypnotic suggestion that every time they feel the grip of the club in their hand, it will be a cue to focus and feel confident before taking the shot.

Post-hypnotic suggestions and cues are outward expressions of the good work that is done in hypnosis. One can resist a post-hypnotic suggestion by choice, but certain negative cues are habitual and can take a bit of working on to shake off. The subconscious will respond to a cue even when the conscious mind has forgotten it completely. This explains why people will unconsciously go out of their way to avoid certain cues that bring up certain sensations.

When we become aware of the different cues that bring out the worst in us, we can then alter their symbolic value by changing our subconscious attitude towards them in hypnosis. In other words, it is easier to replace the response than it is to erase it. For example, if a cigarette is providing a pleasure cue for the smoker, this can be reversed. The new response can be: every time I see or smell a cigarette, it instantly creates an urge to drink water or breathe very deeply until the craving is gone. Now the old unwanted cue has become a pre-arranged response to act appropriately in the face of temptation. The new response replaces the former response to the smoking trigger. In other words, the cue has created a positive substitute and alternative for smoking. If you were to suggest in trance that the next time you smell a cigarette it will make you feel nauseous, this would be a good example of using a cue to bring up a negative response to a post-hypnotic suggestion for the betterment of health.

Post-hypnotic suggestions and cues should be reinforced a number of times in trance before being carried out in reality and a good way to make suggestions more effectual is by using *symbols* to represent desired cues. A symbol is basically anything that stands for something else. Past experiences (memory) can provide us with the symbols that are most significant to us. There are certain symbols that one person is more drawn to than the next. The figure of Christ on the cross could symbolically cue a response in one person to be forgiving. But for the child who was forced to pray for hours on end by a strict parent, the cross could symbolize fear of either a natural Father, God the Father, or both. On encountering a cross in the future, an automatically triggered cue may bring up old feelings and emotions linked to childhood, similar to that of a conditioned reflex. This happens when symbols have not been desensitized properly and is where post-hypnotic suggestions can greatly help reduce sensitivity.

Symbolism has played a vital role in the evolution of mankind's development of thought and explains why we are so naturally attracted to symbols and their meaning. Symbols appear consciously in the mind and in our dreams. Their meaning can be somewhat understood through dream analysis, interpretation and so on. How we gain insight into which symbols provide positive cues for us is by noticing when we encounter them whether they are having a positive or negative effect upon us. If a symbol is providing us with positive cues, then it can be strengthened in hypnosis and made use of in reality through post-hypnotic suggestion. If it is not providing us with positive cues, then its meaning should be altered in hypnosis so that it becomes positive. By exposing our minds to the symbols that affect us, we enlighten the subconscious that they are not objects to be feared anymore. Instead we have a new symbolic meaning in the light of present understanding.

Post-hypnotic suggestions should be specific to your particular goals. If you were going to be sitting an exam, you could give yourself the following suggestion:

"It's May the second, the day of my exam, and I'm feeling relaxed, just as relaxed as I feel now in hypnosis."

Over time you will get used to implanting post-hypnotic suggestions and they will become a vital part of your self-hypnotic experiences. But first you must decide on what positive changes you want in your life.

The Make Up of Your Mind (A Psychoanalytic View)

If you are to make use of the self-hypnotic process you must first have a basic understanding of how the *mind* works within the structure of the *psyche*. *Mind* refers to all aspects of intelligence and consciousness which are manifested as combinations of thought, emotion, perception, memory, will and imagination.

The Psyche

In essence, the *psyche* is the whole of the mind, both *conscious* and *unconscious*. It is every aspect of your thinking and from a philosophical standpoint could be perceived as the *spirit* of a person. Whichever way you percieve your mind, it is personal to you and is based on your life experience.

The Conscious Mind

The *conscious mind* contains all that is inside your awareness and is mostly concerned with logical, rational and civilized thinking. It has control of the *nervous system* and the voluntary actions of the muscles and is the area of your psyche that is most accessible. Because it has the power to accept or reject anything at will, it likes to give us options and choices based on learned experience.

By nature it can be judgmental. But during hypnosis this *critical factor* is *by-passed*, allowing acceptance of an idea, belief, suggestion or image to be programmed into your subconscious without argument. Once an idea has been accepted and takes root in the subconscious, it then must be discharged in the thought or action of the individual.

> "The subconscious mind creates symptoms therefore it is only the subconscious mind that can cure them."
> **Dr. Joseph E. Keaney**

The Subconscious Mind (and/or Unconscious Mind)

The area of the mind that hypnosis utilizes the most is the subconscious. The subconscious has control over the autonomic nervous system, involuntary muscles, organs, glands, and all the other workings of the body structure which we consciously don't have to think about. In the subconscious the sum total of your life experience is recorded in great detail to the present moment. It believes what it is told. And it can only accept, interpret and obey this advice basing its reaction upon information already accepted in the light of its present understanding. The subconscious mind is the center of feelings, thoughts, urges, emotions, impulses and memories that are outside your conscious awareness. It makes no determination or judgment concerning the truth of information it receives because the subconscious simply has no ability to reason. It is very open to suggestion and can react to any given situation with little regard for logic.

The Personal Unconscious

This is the area of your mind that is personal to you. It is a reservoir of information that was once conscious but has been suppressed over time.

The Preconscious

From an analytical standpoint the *preconscious* lies somewhere between your conscious and unconscious. The data that is stored in the preconscious is not conscious, but can be retrieved at your minds leisure, should you wish to view it. Without this region of consciousness, useless information would gather and bombard normal thinking.

The Collective Unconscious

Collective unconscious is a term originally coined by Carl G. Jung. Sigmund Freud didn't distinguish between *individual psychology* and *collective psychology*, but Jung clearly distinguished the *collective unconscious* from the *personal unconscious*. The collective unconscious has also been referred to as "the area of the mind containing experiences." There you experience the remnants of history. A fountain of knowledge, passed down through time." (O'Briain 2008)

The collective unconscious is composed of archetypes. Archetypes are fragments of experience that have been deposited throughout the history of man. It is the age-old region of consciousness, and could be regarded as the essence of the mind.

Libido

Jung believed that *libido* was not just *sexual energy*, as it had been early described by Sigmund Freud, but instead was *psychical energy* that generated in the unconscious and appeared in consciousness in the form of symbols. It is this psychical energy that drives you forward, providing you stay active. But this energy also moves inward, in what Jung described as an *intro-version of the libido*. This is where a person may begin to rely more on inner thoughts, feelings and impulses to satisfy themselves. *Activity* is what drives libido forward naturally. This psychical energy is common to all mankind, like an electrical current passed on through generations.

Like the tide, it moves to and fro upon a seashore of thoughts, feelings and impulses. At times of increased activity, interest and happiness, it vibrantly strives forward on to the land. But when the unconscious drive is weakened through inactivity, or difficult life circumstances, it tends to retreat back to the security of the sea and to the safety of the mother. The developing child learns to adapt to the world without the need for mother's hand, but this infantile longing to be nutured and cared for remains throughout life.

So long as you keep yourself active, so too will the upwardly striving energy in your mind remain active and satisfied. Through desire and interest you create drive, and its momentum is determined by how willing you are to move beyond the limitations and securities of childhood.

Ego

The *ego* is the conscious part of your psyche which you normally identify with. It is your personality and the center of consciousness. It is your identity.

Self

The *self* is the realization that your psyche is constantly striving to fulfill. It is the essence of you and is also the central point to which every other part is related.

Chapter 4

Trancing and Changing

"Change is for the better."
Cathal O'Briain

Hypnosis and Brainwave Activity

The human brain is an *electromagnetic* organ which produces about ten watts of electrical current. With the use of an *EEG* (electroencephalograph) it is possible to measure the patterns of brain waves which fluctuate depending on brain and body activity. These brainwave patterns can be categorized into four primary patterns: *Beta waves, Alpha waves, Theta waves* and *Delta waves*. The *conscious state* produces *beta wave activity*. Because hypnosis works within the other three brainwave classifications *Alpha, Theta* and *Delta*, I will now describe their relation to the three main trance or hypnotic states: the *light trance state*, the *medium trance state*, and the *deep trance state*. It should be noted that the most relevant brainwave in discussing hypnosis is the *alpha*, although all four brainwaves exist to varying degrees. Alpha is usually regarded as the subconscious range. *Meditation* is also in this range, although sometimes it makes use of theta. Dreaming while asleep takes place in theta; *daydreaming* usually occurs in alpha.

The Trance States:

The Light Trance State

The *light trance state* of hypnosis corresponds to the *alpha state*. It is characterized by enhanced physical relaxation, lethargy and eye catalepsy. It stimulates heightened creativity, awareness and high levels of suggestibility. The brain wave patterns of this state are alpha waves, thus the state can be referred to as the *alpha state*. It is in this state that you slip into hypnosis.

It is in this state that you *daydream*, producing brief moments of engrossed inner focusing, where you can slip in and out of light trance from *five to thirty times a minute* without ever knowing it. This explains how you manage to drive your car home with no conscious recall of the details of how you got there. Researchers tell us that the *alpha state* may represent the brain's way of *idling* between states of high mental activity and sleep. While in light trance you feel detached but alert and also experience a definite slowing down of body pulsation. Hypnosis causes the brain to cycle down into alpha without going to sleep. In the alpha state, the subconscious is more open to suggestion.

The Medium Trance State

The *medium trance state* of hypnosis corresponds to the *medium* to *upper* levels of *theta*. At this level of trance you can relive past experiences in greater detail, and suggestibility levels are very high indeed. Smell and taste changes can be observed, and *analgesia* (no pain) along with automatic movements are also noted. Total relaxation is achieved, bringing one to the brink of night-time sleep.

The Deep Trance State

The *deep trance state* of hypnosis corresponds to the *medium* to *upper* levels of *theta*. Suggestibility is now at its highest. As the cycles decrease you enter a state of profound sleep. Now there is even a further slowing down of mental activity and then we start dreaming. In the dream state, we sort out our physical and mental processes. It is a period of rest and rejuvenation, as well as body cell renewal.

Self-Sabotage

Self-sabotage is when you set about foiling your own plans, goals, dreams, etc., usually not knowing why you have done so. If your subconscious was allowed to have its way all the time, it would probably tell you that you *could* or *should* do something else that is easier, or perhaps more comfortable. Here are some examples of self-sabotage:

> *Not going ahead with what you originally set out to do is a classic example.*
>
> *When you give up half way on a dream, you safely put it down to sabotage.*
>
> *When you cannot do something that you really ought to be able to do, this is sabotage.*

Allowing insecurities to control your life, becoming lazy and complacent, or having a negative attitude towards yourself and others, all can be signs of sabotage. They are signs you must learn to recognize. If not kept under control, you end up sabotaging every plan you make, and eventually every thought you think.

Symptom Satisfaction

Change is a positive word. It tells you something exciting and different is happening or about to happen in your life. Making alterations in the present to help fulfil wishes of a better future may appear enough to drive your ambition temporarily. But in order for real, transitional change to occur, you must be willing to make *sacrifices* in your life. In other words, you must be willing to *give up* something, or perhaps many things.

The reality about symptoms is: they provide pleasure and satisfaction on a mental, physical and emotional level. Because satisfaction provides a means of replenishing mental energy, it can make it difficult to give up or sacrifice the very things in life that give you pleasure. Indeed at some level, you enjoy, maintain and protect your symptoms from change. In hypnotherapy, this is called *secondary gain,* and is a common cause of problems. Protecting and nourishing symptoms may appear illogical and unsatisying to the well-adjusted person. But unfortunately it's a common feature in all of us, and a trait which can take on many deceiving and illusionary forms; tricking us into believing that somehow we are changing when we are actually not. In order for real change to occur, you must be willing to *sacrifice the pleasure of staying put in the comfort zone.*

It may come as a shock to realize that you've been deliberately sabotaging your attempts to change up to now. Consciously you may want to change, but subconsciously it may be the very last thing on your mind. Sacrificing pleasure by giving up the comfort of thinking and acting in the same way you've always done, is what establishes the right conditions for change to occur. By not giving in to your deeper mind's every *demand* to nourish symptoms, whether this be through your thoughts, words or actions, you then encourage a healthy, driven desire to manefest in you. This enables energy to be invested productively, instead of being wasted in the maintainence of a symptom.

If symptoms are to be sacrificed, the life-changes being made by the individual must involve *substitute satisfactions*: ones that are equal or more gratifying than the destructive ones currently being used.

The healthier substitutes are found in the external reality that is life. Through social interaction, and healthy, challenging activities, mental energy is encouraged to function normally and beneficially. By acknowledging that certain symptoms are providing satisfaction, you quickly learn to spot-check your thoughts for sabotaging behaviour that only makes you give in to your symptoms demands. By doing so you will begin to recognise the repeated habitual trends that discourage positive change from happening. By not giving in to your symptoms demands, your subconscious will quickly learn that change is good, albeit difficult at times to do. *Desire for change* will become the new demand of your subconscious. A healthy demand that involves activity to satisfy it.

About Conflict

Conflict arises when you prevent yourself from thinking or acting out a desire that is deemed too unpleasant or unethical to remain in normal conscious thought. If an idea or wish is unacceptable to us or society, emotion can be repressed in the form of anger, resentment, guilt, etc. Thoughts of a sexual nature are most likely to create conflict and if this type of repression is deep-rooted, its removal should be left to a professional therapist. But not all conflict becomes repression and some can be resolved by means of identification in self-hypnosis. Through understanding the motivation behind a particular symptom, conflict can be ratio-nalized and removed.

A singer may develop a sore throat before a big performance even though he/she is in perfect health leading up to the day. Consciously they might feel ready for the gig, but at a subcon-scious level there could be motivational forces at work, creating a defense mechanism. Where there was conflict between conscious and subconscious thought, pressure associated with performing may have caused the subconscious to prevent the person from singing by giving them a sore throat. A past experience could be responsible for such a symptom and can only be fixed by letting the subconscious know, through suggestion and imagination, that the singer does not fear the upcoming event.

Accepting Imperfection

If life was perfect you would have nothing to strive for. From an early age some are told to give one hundred per cent and grow up believing that anything less can only spell failure. In the past I have helped clients to resolve emotionally-induced illness only to find them back on my doorstep a few weeks later with a new problem. Symptom substitution and self-sabotage are often the underlying reasons for their return. But hidden behind their behavioural pattern is often an instinctive drive to achieve a new level of *perfection* that can only be found through the manifestation of a new problem. By accepting and believing that we are imperfect, and that life is also, a positive shift in unconscious thinking is made. This acceptance brings us closer to happiness and self-contentment in the present, by removing the idea that perfection will be achieved at some point in the future, providing we continue to struggle towards it.

Life is made up of moments in the here and now, and only the here and now can bring about contentment. Perfection gives rise to the idea that it is faultless. Well, the simple fact is, humans are far from faultless. This is what makes us imperfectly unique and the ones who do well in life are those who can live with imperfection while at the same time making their mark upon an imperfect world. In the material world, simple tools that provide a satisfied state of contentment are often overpowered by the latest commodities on the market that promise to bring us closer in our search for the perfect life. This is an illusion that unfortunately has many under its spell, and tends to make its victims look externally for a happiness that can only be found within. The problem with perfection is that when we think we've reached it, we find a fault. We try and perfect it more, which means that it is no longer perfect. Then we go and look for something else to perfect, eventually finding fault with that also. By regularly implanting the suggestion *"I love and accept the way I am,"* you help your mind to accept imperfection. This can be done both in and out of hypnosis.

Useful Affirmations

A good way to implant suggestion with or without the use of self-hypnosis is through repeated affirmations. Here are a few affirmations that can be used in or out of the hypnotic state. Pick the ones you like or create your own and start using them on a daily basis:

I'm a good person.
I'm clever and creative, talented and trustworthy.
I'm calm and confident, cool and collected.
I'm caring and considerate, kind and comforting.
Everyday is a blessing and life is for living.
I expect to succeed because I'm naturally successful.
I achieve goals easily and effortlessly.
I approve of myself and others approve of me.
Everything I do brings me luck and good fortune.
I expect things to work out for me.
I'm an excellent decision maker.
I enjoy working with people because they enjoy working with me.
Life has much in store for me.
My outlook on life is always positive.

Implanting suggestion both in and out of hypnosis is crucial for keeping your internal programme positive and up to date. By monitoring the way you use suggestion, you enable the subconscious to register and carry out what is practical for healthy living. Now it is paying less attention to insignificant matters that can often occupy the mind. Self-hypnosis is a tool for helping us to solve problems so that we can create a better life. But harnessing the power of the subconscious requires more than just the proper use of suggestion; it also requires willingness on our part to change the manner in which we speak to ourselves. Happy words attract happiness, and melancholy words induce sadness. Your voice is essential to self-hypnosis, and so its language must be clean and positive. In the future I want you to make a special effort to be kind to yourself, making sure at all times to be up-beat with your language and optimistic in your thinking. Give your inner program a real chance to develop and soon enough you will notice your external voice beginning to reflect what you are truly thinking. This means you will no longer have to put up a front. You will come across as confident, genuine and in full control. Peace, harmony, wealth and success are all products of suggestion.

Chapter 5

Mastering the Breath

"When the breath is held, or too fast, hyperventilation naturally occurs. When the breath is free and slow, relaxation naturally occurs. Breathing slowly, steadily and silently is the only way to breathe and is the only way to truly relax."
Cathal O'Briain

Caution! *Always make sure to practice these breathing exercises on an empty stomach. A heavy meal will reduce concentration, causing blood and oxygen to flow to the stomach instead of the brain where it's required. If you suffer with breathing problems, consult a healthcare proffessional immediately!*

About Breathing

If you wish to master the art of self-hypnosis, you first must learn to breathe properly. The breath is essential for inducing the hypnotic state. This is something that is not always emphasized enough by those who teach self-hypnosis.

"To draw air into and expel it from the lungs." This is the definition you will find in the *Oxford Dictionary* if you look up the word *breathe*. Although it's common knowledge that one needs to breathe air in order to stay alive, you must also recognize that breathing is far more than simply drawing air in and expelling it out. It is the most essential tool at your disposal for creating in your mind and body a sense of well-being, especially when dealing with aspects of living such as stress management. It is a function of the body that works both voluntarily and involuntarily. Contrary to the dictionary explanation, a true breath is

54

firstly created by *exhaling slowly and completely*. The reason we begin the breath by exhaling is because in order for an object to be filled, it first must be emptied. Removing tainted impure air through the *out-breath* allows your lungs to be filled completely with fresh air when the time comes to inhale. Although people naturally tend to breathe in first, whenever you wish to consciously breathe for relaxation purposes, etc. the breath should begin by exhaling, followed by inhaling. This allows you to inhale a complete lung full of fresh, pure air. The *out-breath* triggers the parasympathetic nervous system: *the relaxation response*. The *in-breath* triggers the sympathetic nervous system: *the arousal response*. The out-breath should always be longer than the in-breath. The difference in time should be about eleven seconds for exhaling and seven seconds for inhaling. By breathing out slower and longer you increase the relaxation response. In doing so, you also decrease the *arousal response*.

Breathing and Self-Awareness

Breathing is an unconscious activity just like any other natural phenomenon, such as blood circulation or food digestion. But in times of increased physical or mental stress its rhythm is affected. When presented with stressful or difficult environ-ments, very often a person will begin to hold their breath and as a result fail to breathe normally. Thoughts of a fearful nature have the ability to encourage poor breathing. It is in these times of increased mental and physical stress that we need to be even more aware of our breathing than normal. It is therefore important to raise our levels of self-awareness each time we come into contact with stress, whether internal or external. This is achieved by *spot-checking*.

Spot-Checking

Spot-checking is done by noticing if you are holding your breath, taking short little breaths, or breathing faster than is necessary for the given situation. If you are doing any of these, it's now time to switch to a conscious and deliberate mode of controlled breathing. The way to breathe steadily and completely is by using the correct breathing technique.

The Correct Breathing Technique

This technique is very useful for concentrating your mind upon your breathing. Take your time learning it and enjoy the way it makes you feel. This is your first step on the road to self-discovery through self-hypnosis. Find somewhere quiet and comfortable to practice and remember; this is your time now.

Exhale slowly, smoothly, silently and completely through the nose.
Expel all the air out of your lungs and contract your belly.
Now pause. Neither inhale nor exhale for a few moments.
Wait until your lungs naturally demand the air.
Inhale slowly, smoothly, silently and completely through the nose.
Allow your belly to rise until you are full.
Do not hold your breath when you are full.
Exhale slowly, smoothly, silently and completely through the nose.
Expel all the air out of your lungs and contract your belly.
Pause. Neither inhale nor exhale for a few moments.
Wait until your lungs naturally demand the air.

The breath should be one whole sequence from start to finish. Do not hold your breath in between inhaling and exhaling as some practitioners recommend. Holding the breath is unnatural, unhealthy and achieves nothing. If you get light-headed you may be approaching the technique too forcefully. Slow down and think of the words *smoothly and silently*. While you are consciously breathing you shouldn't be able to hear yourself inhaling and exhaling, for when the breath is silent it automatically slows down. If you can hear yourself breathe, you are breathing *too fast* and *too forcefully*.

The Correct Breathing Technique (Explained)

Air is expelled from the lungs by exhaling slowly, smoothly, silently and completely. This action is aided by the contraction of the abdominal muscles, expelling any last traces of air. Allow this important exhalation to happen with ease. The more of this air that is expelled from the lungs, the greater the amount of pure fresh air that is received when inhaling. Now you must pause and wait for your breath to come naturally because you feel you need it. This is the only time that the breath is held, not after inhaling, but before inhaling.

Now the breath is drawn through the nose, and the diaphragm lowers itself while the bottom sections of the lungs fill with air. At the same time the abdomen swells out with the rising of the belly. The belly remains inflated until the last stage of exhalation.

After the lower sections of the lungs are filled, the middle sections receive air by expanding and raising the ribs. Now you are almost full to capacity.

By raising the collar-bones and lifting the shoulders, optimum lung capacity is achieved. Lower, middle, and upper sections are now ready for exhalation.

Now You Exhale in this Order:

Lower the collar-bones.
Relax the rib cage.
Contract the belly, pause.

Now the diaphragm returns to its normal position. When the diaphragm has done its job, there are a few crucial moments of respite you must allow before drawing in your second breath. Remember this is the one and only time that the breath is held. It is when you have fully exhaled, and before you inhale, not the other way around. Relaxation in the region can only be felt when the abdominal muscles are at rest. It is at this moment of *respite* between the breaths, when you are neither inhaling nor exhaling, that relaxation is most felt throughout your body. After waiting a few seconds in this period of respite, the air will automatically and naturally want to enter your lungs. The pause between breaths is essential in correct breathing. The ribs, intercostals and chest muscles only have a limited amount of room to expand. This is why you must breathe diaphragmatically, for when the diaphragm is lowered through the action of the abdominal muscles, pulling it downward, the lungs then have more room to expand at the base.

You may be thinking that this seems like a lot of work to do in order to take a single breath. But in time this will become a simple and effective way for you to achieve full respiratory potential, thus increasing your quality of life. A good way to rehearse the correct breathing technique is in the lying down position without using a pillow. A pillow may hinder the passage of air through the windpipe. The best place for your pillow is under the knees. If you can lie down on a carpet floor instead of a bed when learning, a firm support is preferable. When you feel you are proficient at it and understand its method well, you can break down the detailed explanation of how it works into this easier format for remembering.

The Correct Breathing Technique (Simplified)

Exhale, contract belly, pause

(a) Inhale, belly rising

(b) Ribs rising

(c) Collar-bones and shoulders rising

(a) Now exhale, shoulders and collar-bones relaxing

(b) Then ribs

(c) Then belly, pause

Take Your Time

Learning to breathe consciously and correctly takes a while to master. At the beginning you may encounter some resistance from the muscles that are involved, particularly the intercostals between the ribs. But within a few days, through continued expansion and relaxation, these muscles gradually stretch, allowing for sufficient space to breathe in a comfortable manner.

As you practice slow, smooth, silent and complete breathing on your back, bear in mind that it's done in three separate sections. Each section of the respiratory apparatus must be concentrated on individually and in succession. This is how the sections are divided up:

Abdominal (*breathing from the diaphragm*)
Intercostal (*breathing from the ribs*)
Clavicular (*breathing from the top of lungs*)

Incorrect Breathing

Some people make the mistake of pulling in their bellies when inhaling because they think this will help move the air up into their lungs. Contracting the abdominal muscles while inhaling is the incorrect way to breathe. Relaxing the region and allowing it to fill up naturally by flattening the diaphragm and letting your belly rise is the correct way to breathe. This lets the air fill the base of the lungs. When your belly has fully inflated, it should remain that way until the final phase of exhalation.

In the past I have observed people holding in their stomachs when trying their best to disguise their weight. On occasion I've even witnessed men doing this even when they were already in good physical shape. I can only conclude that they do this to accentuate their upper body, thus drawing attention to their chests instead of their stomachs. Women are also guilty of this sucking in of the belly when seeking to draw more attention to their upper body. This painful procedure, often driven by self-consciousness, should be avoided at all costs by those seeking to breathe correctly. It's a contradiction of sorts. On one hand the person contracting their stomach does it to look well and feel confident. But on the other, it's hard to feel confident and relaxed when you can't breathe properly. Sucking in the belly and holding the breath restricts air flow, causing the brain and nervous system to send the wrong signals. The body only tightens up when oxygen can't reach the muscles. A lack of clarity in thought is felt when the breath is held forcefully like this. These, along with a multitude of other side effects, are brought on by sucking in the belly for the sake of looking well to the observer. God has made you the way you are. If people can't derive pleasure from looking at you, well frankly it's their problem and they'll just have to live with it.

Breathing Through Your Nose

Correct breathing is done through the nose because the nose has a filter which warms up the air as it passes into the lungs. Your nostrils also help control the speed flow of the air. If you find it difficult to breathe through your nose, perhaps because of a sinus condition, you can alternatively use your mouth, although it is not the most recommended method of breathing. You often hear health practitioners say, "In through the nose and out through the mouth." But from now on I want you to think, "In through the nose and out through the nose."

By breathing out through the nose, air is just as controlled leaving your lungs, as it was going in. It also means you are not expelling it too quickly. This helps you to focus on the different sections of your lungs being used because of the measured control and concentration you are applying. Taking breaths in and out through the nose can also help disguise the fact that you are consciously breathing to the onlooker. For example, in an interview situation or addressing a large group of people where the nerves might be heightened, breathing in and out through the nose is an effective way to clear the thoughts and relax the body. Now you can settle into your environment without any fear of self-consciousness. By breathing slowly, smoothly, silently and completely, an instantaneous calmness comes over you, paving the way for clear thoughts and actions.

First you start by *spot-checking* your breathing and then you apply the *correct breathing technique*. In doing this you have taken the first step in normalizing your mental and physical reactions to any given situation. Now you are centered, focused and uninhibited by the stress and fatigue that normally accompanies incorrect breathing. Instead of your breath making a stressful situation worse, it now acts as a bridge over troubled waters, a catalyst between environment and clear thought.

When the mind and body have been stabilized through the breath, it is then that we introduce the power of positive suggestion.

Breathing with Positive Suggestion

I like the positive suggestion *calm and relaxed*. These words can be utilized to the full when applied to the breath. An important thing to remember when breathing with positive suggestion is to slow down and broaden the words as you say them in your mind.

Exercise in Breathing with Positive Suggestion

Exhale slowly, smoothly, silently and completely, pause.
Inhale and say the word **calm** *in your mind.*
Exhale and say the words **and relaxed** *in your mind, pause and repeat.*

Exercise in Regaining Control

Exhale slowly, smoothly, silently and completely, pause.
Inhale and say the word **calm** *in your mind.*
Exhale and say the words **and in full control** *in your mind, pause and repeat.*

When we breathe and imagine words simultaneously, the

subconscious registers our desired intentions to a much greater degree than in normal conscious thought. This is because the breath opens the door to your subconscious. When the door is open, suggestion can now be implanted at a deeper level. The subconscious is more open to suggestion than the conscious part of your mind. By concentrating on your breath, the critical and judgmental conscious is by-passed. When we breathe deeply, the subconscious naturally begins to come to the fore. It's in this frame of mind that positive words sink deeply and have greatest effect. Whatever words you choose to suggest and imagine is entirely up to you. Different environments call for different suggestions to suit the frame of mind you wish to be in. But for the moment try and keep the words calm and relaxed as your core suggestion. Here are some other words you may find useful when breathing with positive suggestion:

(Inhale) **Cool,**	*(Exhale)* **and confident**
(Inhale) **I am,**	*(Exhale)* **so calm**
(Inhale) **Full of life,**	*(Exhale)* **full of energy**
(Inhale) **So calm,**	*(Exhale)* **so quiet now**
(Inhale) **Sharp,**	*(Exhale)* **and focused**
(Inhale) **Willing,**	*(Exhale)* **and able**
(Inhale) **Relaxed,**	*(Exhale)* **and ready**

When you practice breathing with positive suggestion, self-hypnosis at its most basic level moves from the confines of the home into the external environment. All that is required to make it work is belief in the suggestions and images you are giving yourself. So when you say words like *calm and relaxed*, say them with belief, emotion, imagination, and expectancy. Very soon your deeper mind will grow accustomed to your truest intentions.

Relaxing the Face Helps Breathing

When we concentrate for long periods of time without relaxing our eyes and face, diaphragmatic breathing gets weakened and the oxygen supply to the brain decreases. If you work in a job that requires you to stare intensely at a computer screen all day or something similar, make sure to look away from what you are concentrating on every ten minutes or so. While you do this, allow your face muscles to fall into repose. Unclench your teeth and let your jaw sag. Do this for twenty seconds and then return to what you were concentrating on. When the eyes and face are relaxed, so is the abdomen. The diaphragm functions more efficiently when intensity of concentration and muscle tone is lessened.

Consciously Sighing for Tension Relief

When you sigh or yawn, it's a basic indication that you're not getting enough oxygen. This is quite a normal physical response and can be utilized for the purpose of relaxation and tension relief. The main thing when practicing this technique is to create a sound while you exhale. This can be achieved by concentrating your attention on the voice box during the out-breath. Although it's correct to breathe out slowly, this is one exercise where you'll find the breath leaving your body quickly enough. This breathing exercise is good because it closely resembles unconscious sighing, which is a natural and healthy activity.

Expel the air from your lungs.
Inhale smoothly and fill your lungs to capacity.
Now exhale and sigh at the same time.

Breathing Life into Your Heart

This is a wonderful way to increase pleasant physiological responses in the mind and body. The idea is to draw on external forces by imagining that outside your body is a source of healing power that is unique to you. This force may be perceived as energy, a white or golden ball of light, the Holy Spirit, or any other representation that is pleasing to you. This breathing technique can be applied for relaxation, increasing energy and spiritual enhancement. But it's also very useful for inducing and deepening the hypnotic state. This is how it's done:

> *Expell the air from your lungs.*
> *As you inhale, imagine an external life force passing in through your nose, down through your neck and into your heart.*
> *Now exhale and imagine the life-force spreading out from your heart, like a gentle ripple in a pool. Repeat.*

Breathing Through Pursed Lips (Prolonging the Relaxation Response)

The aim is to prolong the *relaxation response* by slowing down the *out-breath* even more using pursed lips, as if you are blowing air into the top of a straw. This is a very practical way of bringing about instant relaxation. Just make sure to release the air as slowly and as quietly as possible, as if you are slowly deflating a balloon.

Exercise in Breathing from the Chest (Tension Remover)

> *Exhale slowly, smoothly, silently and completely, pause.*
> *Inhale silently allowing your belly to rise, followed by your chest.*
> *Feel your chest moving up and out.*
> *Let your shoulders fall back while you inhale.*
> *Now exhale through purseds lips as slowly as possible till your lungs are empty, allowing for those crucial moments of respite between the breaths and repeat.*

Breathing and Self-Hypnosis

At the heart of self-hypnosis is the breath that creates it. Without the breath self-hypnosis would be lacking the most essential ingredient it needs in order for it to be effective. By learning how to control our breathing, the power of the breath can be utilized to the full and it's this very power that opens the channel to the deeper part of your mind. When the subconscious fountain of knowledge has been reached through the breath, wisdom is then revealed to us. Here we come in touch with ourselves in the true sense of the word as we are no longer *self-critical*. Mind and body are as one, sustained by the breath, where conscious untruths no longer intrude the pathways of clear understanding. A detachment takes place where judgmental thinking is left to rest while the uncritical observer quietly listens to answers as they come up from the subconscious.

If you are to make full use of your respiratory system and gain as much of its potential as you can, it's important that you practice until such time as it becomes second nature. It may take a couple of days to master as it requires a level of patience on your behalf, but if you set aside some time each day to practice, fifteen minutes or so, soon you will be proficient in the art of correct breathing. Even when you grow accustomed to its methodology and function, continue to practice it in its most basic form. It's easy to slip back into old habits, so be on the look out by reminding yourself to *spot-check* and practice.

Some people get a bit of a shock when they realize that they have been breathing incorrectly most of their lives, but they can take some reassurance in the knowledge that so have most of us. I don't recall it being part of my physical education class in school, and if it was, lessons were probably taught incorrectly. Even if you had been taught how to breathe correctly in school, there's a good chance you would have forgotten it back in those earlier years with more important things on your mind like growing up.

If you wish to be successful at self-hypnosis you must first learn to give up the poor breathing habits that have developed over the years. This is done by *spot-checking* regularly.

When practicing the correct breathing technique, pick a room where you have peace and quiet. Open the window for a few minutes and allow fresh air to circulate, but then close it to keep out the drafts. Take off your shoes, jewelry and your belt as it will only hinder abdominal breathing. Lie on the floor with a pillow under your knees, rest your elbows on the floor, and place your hands gently on the sides of your belly. Don't cross your fingers over each other as the weight of joined hands will stop your belly rising as it should. By placing your hands on your stomach it will help you to feel the expansion in the abdomen as the air fills the bottom of your lungs. When you have practiced feeling the air swelling the lower section, place your hands up higher on your rib-cage to feel the expansion there. Finally place your hands on your collar bones to feel the expansion in the clavicular region. Remember to operate each section of the breathing apparatus in succession and exhale first by contracting the abdominal muscles to squeeze out any last traces of air. In no time you'll have it off to a tee, but no matter how good you get, remember, always *spot-check*.

Breathing as a Form of Distraction and Narrowed Attention

In times of increased stress when external factors or internal anxieties disrupt your mode of breathing, you must spot-check and allow yourself to breathe in a controlled manner by narrowing your attention to your breathing. Concentrating your attention on one thing only, your breathing, acts as a distraction from the thoughts that are bothering you. By diverting your attention to your breath you accomplish two things. Firstly you are thinking of your breath and not of the thought that is causing stress, and secondly you allow yourself to relax completely through the breath.

So the next time you are feeling anxious or stressed about something, settle yourself down by narrowing your attention to how the breath is functioning inside you. By channeling your thoughts to the way you are breathing, your mind will begin to focus and clear. Now your subconscious is in a position to do its job properly, which is to relax you and pass up the answers to the things that have been troubling you.

The conscious part of your mind that you use everyday is brilliant but at the same time limited and should be used for what it is good at, logic, rationalizing, reasoning, language and so on. The subconscious on the other hand is the seat of your emotions, imagination and memory, with the capacity to record all of your life experiences and the power to direct energy. It is intuitive, creative and regulates all the involuntary functions of the body. When the breath is controlled correctly and attention is narrowed on its slow and smooth deliverance, the subconscious can fulfill its purpose in the heightened sense, with better memory, emotional understanding and balance of thought. The breath is the key to heightened subconscious thought, and narrowed attention is the key to distraction from critical conscious thought.

Exercise in Breathing and Narrowed Attention

Lie down in a comfortable position and allow your mind and body to relax.

Focus on a fixed point in the room, perhaps one straight above you on the ceiling.

Your eyes should be under no strain.

This can be achieved by looking neither up nor down but straight ahead.

While you stare, think about your breathing and the way it is moving inside.

Imagine all the sections as they fill up and follow the breath's direction.

When you are satisfied that you are breathing correctly, allow your eyes to gently close. Continue to think about your breathing only and how it is moving inside you.

Spend a while thinking about your breath and when you are finished say in your mind:

"On the count of three I am fully aware and fully alert."

Then count slowly from one to three. On three, open your eyes and have a stretch.

The above exercise will help distract you from conscious thought while you relax your mind and body. Although this exercise was done in the lying down position with your eyes closed, it can be used anywhere and at any time with your eyes open. All you have to do is focus in on your breathing and think of nothing else but how the breath is moving inside you. When you have relaxed yourself through the breath, then you can start applying the suggestion, *calm and relaxed*, while you inhale and exhale.

The Power of Breathing

Correct breathing is the simplest way to focus the mind, relax the body, settle the stomach and calm the nerves. When the breath is allowed to flow freely, its amazing connective power triggers the subconscious to send up the answers you seek. So instead of battling with our conscious mind to find a solution to a problem, it is given to you by that deeper and more knowledgeable part of your mind which knows the answer to every question. The breath reveals an inner truth that helps you to know yourself mentally, physically and spiritually and should no longer be taken for granted as just another unconscious activity of the body.

The ability you have to create a breath is with you from birth, but through internal and external distractions, family and social problems, it becomes less effective as time passes, and it is because of this there must develop a need in you to bring your breath back to its full potential. When re-mastered, its power for *self-healing* is yours for the taking. It has been proven beyond doubt that incorrect breathing can cause illness and worsen existing illness. So make it your friend and not your foe by harnessing its strength through self-awareness. *Spot-check* the rhythm of your breathing on a daily basis and allow yourself a little time each day to practice *the correct breathing technique.* You will notice other changes happening too like memory improvement and vocal expression. *Breathing with positive suggestion* is the best way to practice self-hypnosis in the waking state and can be performed anywhere, at any time.

Breathe life into your lungs today and take your first steps on the healing path of self-hypnosis. There is no time like the present to start breathing correctly, because when you have found peace in your mind, body and soul, it shows on your face and in your actions, where a breath of air all of a sudden becomes a breath of life.

Remember, even at the best of times, you can lose touch with your breath, holding on to it, or breathing too fast. In order to stay relaxed, you must remain connected to the *relaxation response*, and this is done through use of the *out-breath.* Breathing in slowly is most important, for when we breathe in too fast it only maintains and strengthens the connection to the *flight or flight* response. Always make sure to let all the air out of your lungs, slowly, smoothly and completely, and when you have done so, wait. Wait until your lungs naturally demand the air to come back into your body. Correct breathing is correct thinking, and when you are in control of your breath, you are also in control of your mind and body.

Chapter 6

Imagination, Visualization and Solution-Focused Therapy

"Whether the image is good, bad, or indifferent, it tends to become realized."
Cathal O'Briain

From Imagination to Reality

The word *imagination* comes from the Latin word *imaginare* which means to form an image, or to represent. It is one of the most important, creative aspects of the human mind. When you use your imagination in self-hypnosis, you are giving the subconscious a canvas on which to paint your desired self-image. The deeper mind perceives you the way you perceive yourself. If you paint a poor self-image, it can only create a behavioral program to suit that very image. So it is important that you must always visualize yourself looking and acting your natural best. As I mentioned earlier, the subconscious believes anything it is told. The same goes for anything it sees. So whenever you present it with a picture of a confident and self-assured person, it then goes about creating a behavioral program to suit that very image.

Everything is experienced in the imagination as if it were *real*, even though imagination is an *unreal* state of mind. Imagination borders alongside conscious reality and is the most easily accessed point from consciousness. This is why there is a fine line between *what you perceive as real*, and what in fact is: *the product of your imagination*.

In the imagination you build up images to be carried out in reality. The more you dwell upon these images, the greater their chance becomes of being realized. Everything you desire must be imagined first. The more you exercise your imagination actively, the quicker you get results. A boxer on entering the ring before a big fight cannot afford to neglect his imagination. Nor does he imagine the possibility of being knocked out, because if he did, he would almost certainly hit the canvas. What he imagines is winning each consecutive round perfectly (process imagery), and then holding the trophy at the end of the fight (result imagery).

If your dreams do not manifest themselves into reality it is because you have chosen to keep them locked inside your imagination in the form of fantasy. The way to make your imagination work for you is to acknowledge and appreciate its power. By realizing that your imagination has the capacity to turn you into whatever you wish to be, you have taken an important step on the road to *self-realization*. Fearful images get replaced by desired images and this is what actively projects you forward.

You must not fear the power and ability you have. But rather you must control and direct it. This is done by making clear and continuingly repeating images that you wish to make real. If your desire is to have a successful interview, you must see the interview room clearly in your mind; imagine its shape and size; notice the smell of the furniture; feel the grip of your friendly handshake; visualize the chair you will sit in; hear yourself talking with confidence and then make this picture bright and colorful in your mind's eye. When you have done this, play the image over again as vividly as you can, involving as many of your *five senses* as possible. The more senses you involve, the better the quality of the image. The better the quality of the image, the quicker it becomes realized.

Why Imagination is so Important

Einstein once said, "Imagination is more powerful than knowledge." It is what allows you to see and shape any scenario that you wish to make real. If you don't like your reality, you must change your mental images. By changing your mental images, you change your reality. Here are the main reasons why imagination is so important:

Imagination creates the potential for success by showing the mind your truest intentions.

Imagination helps you view many possibilities without relying on one logical answer.

Imagination has the power to create any sensation felt or about to be felt.

Creative or active visualization is the ability to productively use your imagination.

It is how you turn images into reality.

The more feeling emotion you attach to an image, the quicker it manifests into reality.

Images with emotion have potent energy, especially when you involve your senses.

Imagination attracts that which you desire.

The opportunities present themselves.

Imagination has unlimited power, providing of course you don't limit your imagination.

If you keep imagining the same thing, and keep thinking the same thoughts, other people unconsciously act upon your thoughts.

Thoughts and powerful imaginings have the ability to travel from one mind to another.

This bolsters your position for attracting success, for others are now also working on your behalf.

Using Imagination Wisely

From the moment you wake up it is important to render images of a happy, confident and relaxed person. The reason some people look so unhappy is not always down to the circumstances they are in. Sometimes it's simply because of the negative way they use their imagination to perceive themselves. On looking out the window, a person may see rain and automatically begin visualizing themselves looking sad and depressed, basing their mood on past experiences of how they felt on rainy days. Because they associate bad weather with images of feeling low, their subconscious is automatically given a picture of how they think they should act and feel. And so, they become the product of their own imagery. Environmental changes should not determine your mood, but unfortunately for some, they do. It's easy to blame the weather for feeling low, but you only have yourself to blame when you allow your imagination to get the better of you.

If a negative image pops into your head, a good way to decrease its power is to take the color and vividness out of it. This is done by changing the image from color to black and white and then shrinking it down in size until it is very small in your mind's eye. Now it can be thrown into an imaginary skip and burned if that is your wish. This negative image should then be replaced by a big, clear, positive and colorful one. It's a simple but very effective way to rid your imagination of negative images.

The imagination is like a bridge between conscious and subconscious thought. If you use it wisely, these two areas of the mind can develop a better relationship of trust. The conscious is less critical when it experiences repetitive ideas through image. If the subconscious is passing up images of a positive, consistent nature, it leaves less room for mental conflicts to emerge between the two areas of thinking. So it's important that you imagine the same positive images in the waking state, as you do in self-hypnosis. You must keep your imagination free of negative images that only contradict your deepest desires. In times of stress you must breathe with positive suggestion while using your imagination actively and wisely.

Solution-Focused Therapy

When *conflict* has its origin in the subconscious, the solution can be most likely found there too. *Solution-focused therapy* includes a number of techniques and interventions, all of which are implemented in order to bring about a complete lasting solution. It encourages you to put into effect what is already working and the aim is to utilize solutions that bring about positive life changes rather than dwelling on problems the mind has already exhausted. The solution must be desired and imagined first. By working out a personalized plan of therapy to be practiced on a daily basis, a foundation can be laid for a new behavioral program to develop through imagination.

Solution-focused therapy makes full use of the existing skills and resources already within you. However, a shift in thinking is required, especially for the person who is problem-focused by nature.

You must ask the question, "What changes do I want and how soon do I want them?"

If your wish is to have greater self-confidence, your subconscious must become aware of this intention and the time frame in which you will achieve it. Set about incorporating the ideas and techniques you learn in this book, so that after a short time they become second nature to you. The mind adapts quickly providing there is willingness to change and this process is speeded up where there is a belief in your own skills and self-hypnotic capabilities. Throughout the day special attention must always be given to the breath, suggestion, and imagination.

The notion of one step forward and two steps back is a misconception of how reality actually unfolds. If you encounter a setback on the road to good health, consider it a call to action and revert back to self-hypnosis and *solution-focused self-therapy*. Setbacks are to be viewed as learning experiences from which you gain better insight into yourself. When the subconscious has learnt that it can recover from a setback, you are then in a much better position to face whatever life may throw you, knowing that you will always recover. A relaxed mind is better able to find solutions. When the mind learns to be still, creativity and positive emotional response to imagination is heightened. Now your focus is on desired objects, and that is what attracts them to you. But in order to be in tune with your emotions and capabilities, you must remind yourself daily not to become complacent about doing such basic things as maintaining a good self-image. Solution-focused therapy combines all the elements of natural self-healing. You have simply taken responsibility for your thoughts by making a conscious decision to change old negative beliefs into new positive ones, through imagination.

"Solution Focused therapy involves programming the 'auto-pilot'
in the subconscious mind to achieve its destination
and desired outcome."
Dr. Joseph E. Keaney

Solution-Focused Daily Plan (Basic)

Morning time:
Sit down and take 10, very slow, very deep breaths.
Take 10 more breaths only this time incorporating the suggestion,
*   calm and relaxed, while you breathe with positive suggestion.*
Now imagine your day as you wish it to unfold (process imagery).
Visualize yourself at different times throughout the day and keep
*   these images positive and intentional.*
Imagine what you are going to be doing at the end of the day (result
*   imagery) and how you are going to look and feel.*

Solution-Focused Daily Plan (Explained)

The breath is what helps to shake off sleep and can easily clear the mind after a long night of dreaming. On awakening from sleep we often drift into the day lacking in energy, carrying with us feelings that are only there because of the dreams we've had.

After taking twenty deep breaths you feel alive and motivated, centered and focused. You feel refreshed, energized and as though you've not been asleep. This is when you should empower your subconscious with simple, effective suggestions such as, full of life, full of energy, sharp and focused, cool and confident, all in conjunction with the breath. Energy promoting suggestions can be implanted and felt within seconds.

Say it, imagine it, believe it, and feel it.

Now imagine how you want the day to unfold using process imagery. Visualize your desired intentions, exactly the way you want them to look in reality. See yourself in your mind's eye at 10.00am, 12.00pm, 3.00pm, and 5.00pm and so on. If you are someone who gets stressed driving a car, imagine briefly that you are driving home in rush hour looking very relaxed behind the wheel. See yourself eating at the dinner table. And then imagine what the end of the day will look like. This is result imagery, the result being that you go to bed happy, acknowledging that you've had a wonderful day. Visualize yourself sleeping soundly that night. By pre-empting your day before it has actually unfolded you give your subconscious a preview of the future and how you desire it to look. Although your day may not always turn out exactly how you imagined, by actively imagining it before it has happened, you greatly increase the likelihood of living out your day the way you want. You shape reality instead of reality shaping you. It only takes ten minutes to do in the morning and is a routine well worth getting into. It's you taking charge of mental health by giving yourself some gentle and relaxing treatments similar to getting a facial or having your back massaged. Only with matters of the mind, mental and physical care should be more ongoing and necessary.

Internalizing at the Correct Pace

In the same way you *spot-check* your breathing, so too should you *spot-check* your thoughts for signs of over indulgence within a particular thought or thoughts. Information can be regurgitated over and over with the same idea being spontaneously worked through, regardless of the fact that a satisfactory conclusion may have been reached already. This can happen for a number of reasons. The idea may not have been fully accepted by the subconscious and so remains conscious for further analysis. It could be habit. Or you may have made countless observations regarding the obsessive thought, but through ritualistic behavior your conscious inner voice may be telling you that the matter has not yet been resolved and must be scrutinized and inspected further. There could also be a dynamic value behind your commitment to rethinking the same thought over and over. Internalizing about a particular problem may be providing a scapegoat for avoiding the real underlying conflict that has yet to be addressed, where the more you obsess about trivial matters, the less you have to think about the real issues in need of inspection.

When under any kind of stress, special attention must be paid to slowing down your breath and pace you are internalizing at. When the brain is relaxed, the mind naturally aspires to fulfill dreams. Imagination then becomes more active as you encounter the flow experience, where one pleasant thought sparks another in natural succession.

As children, personality develops through exploration of *fantasy, thought* and *image*. Imagination runs wild creating the self-image, moving the child constantly towards ever changing images. As children we are the true masters of turning fantasy into reality and with no time to ponder on thoughts that provoke anxiety, we simply avoid them in the fantasy state. But as adults it gets that bit harder to avoid directed thinking, especially concerning matters of the heart or financial worry. But by simply recognizing that you are dwelling too much upon a particular thought, you start to bring yourself back into the realm of productive imaginary thinking. You can do this through breathing with positive suggestion. By using the suggestion, *calm and relaxed*, in conjunction with deep controlled breathing, clarity of thought is soon felt which in turn gives rise to suitable conditions for fantasy thinking.

Creative energy is brought about by an active and interested imagination that works in harmony with the rest of the mind. This creative energy is similar to that of a burning desire to produce a work of art or write a poem. The breath helps you sustain an active imagination and imagination is what helps us to internalize in a healthy and energy promoting manner. The pace at which you internalize affects the pace at which you verbalize. The inner voice and outer voice that express thought can work with or against each other. When the voice has become a poor vehicle for what the mind wishes to express, attention must be given once again to bringing about a settling in thought. This is done by internalizing at the correct pace through the breath, suggestion and imagination.

Instilling a Positive Self-Image

Imagine for a moment what you would look like if you were at your natural best. How would you walk, talk and behave? Visualize your mannerisms and your body language. The *self-image* you have just created within a matter of seconds is exactly the type you must implant in your subconscious on a daily basis. While in self-hypnosis you can make these self-images big, bright, bold and colorful. If you have any difficulty in trying to imagine what you look like at your natural best, think of someone you know who loves you unconditionally. Think about what it is that they really love and respect about you. This will help you to identify and gain a better understanding of the qualities people love about you.

Overcoming fear by doing precisely what it is you fear strengthens the poor self-image. Fear must be kept for when it is only truly necessary and should not be spread thinly throughout the body in the form of anxiety as it often is. The self-image must be free of fear. Instilling a good self-image has little to do with vanity but more to do with self-respect.

The Mirror Technique

A good way to imprint a clear and positive self-image in your imagination is to use a mirror. This technique is useful for painting a strong picture in your subconscious of how you want your self-image to be in reality.

Look at yourself in the mirror.

Strike a pose of how you desire to look; smile, laugh, look confident, and so on.

Close your eyes and see the imprint in your imagination. Repeat.

The Process of Change through Desire and Interest

Throughout the ages the ever evolving mind has enjoyed the fruits of change and self-development. Man's exploration into the workings of the psyche has revealed a mind that naturally aspires to reach new levels of self-awareness. Change is constant and seeks to attain individual purpose within a meaningful life. It likes to work harmoniously within universal law and is quite subtle in its movements, but it also has the ability to leave a person stuck in the past or move them swiftly along in the present.

Unconscious acceptance of change comes through a belief that change is beneficial, safe and achievable. One might consciously want change but unconsciously fear it. So it's really about convincing the unconscious that change is desirable. Some people experience change by drifting in and out of the *comfort zone*. It's that bit easier to sail through uncharted waters when you have the safety net of the comfort zone to fall back into. But real change comes about when the comfort zone is abandoned completely by allowing ourselves the privilege of moving forward and not looking back. By not looking back, I mean that you must not invest energy in the past, but rather in what you desire in the present. It is *desire* and *interest* in the present that motivates your mind to change and mature. When strong desire attracts something new into your life, it helps the process of change to be accelerated through belief and expectancy. You can easily learn to long for a cigarette or a cold bottle of beer within a short period of time. This type of longing you experience comes through desire and interest. The same longing can be applied to bring about positive change and spiritual growth. If what you are doing is not interesting or stimulating you, a change of scenery may be in order.

Keep your mind active and its programming precise through simple, driven language. Believe in your subconscious, for it's a lot older than you. Centuries of experience make up the subconscious and the answers to most questions can be found there. A longing for inner peace and wisdom is a worthy virtue. A longing for God will bring you closer to Him. Whether you long for the material or the spiritual, the process of change is heightened and accelerated through desire and interest.

Trusting Your Intuition

The subconscious guides you best when you trust in its ability to instinctively direct and shape your present through imagination. Going with the gut feeling helps to overcome fear of the unknown. The subconscious is not reckless and recognizes danger even before it presents itself. So real fear and unrealistic fear must be separated by doing what intuitively feels right. Here you become involved in the flow experience, where thoughts and beliefs are filled with purpose and meaningful intent. You have answered the call of your heart by trusting your mind's deep intuitive wisdom. The first thought, feeling or reaction is often the right one, especially if you have a positive imagination. This doesn't mean that logical consideration has been ignored; only that intuition has paved the way for clearer understanding. How often did your first impression of someone turn out to be right? Remember all the times you felt danger in your midst, where you had a knowing, a sense of things. We are all intuitive when we want to be, but many of us keep this natural skill in reserve. Negative thinking can weaken the mind, so listen carefully to your inner voice, checking its language and watching its pace, slowing it down with the breath. By maintaining a relaxed frame of mind, the subconscious helps you because you are working with it instead of against it. Trusting it to provide the answers you need saves on mental energy and reduces fatigue.

As you learn to relax, so too do you develop intuitiveness. In a relaxed state, the subconscious comes to the fore and this allows for greater insight. The more relaxed you are, the more intuitive you become. *Light trance* can be easily induced through concentration and relaxation and this can be done at regular intervals throughout the day. When using trance in conversation, your voice becomes clearer and your body language reflects what you are thinking and saying. There is open dialogue and healthy conscious debate within an active mind, where thoughts give rise to more thoughts and don't become too fixated. Freedom of thought is freedom of expression and freedom of expression is trusting intuition.

Creative Play

Staying mentally positive and physically active is taking responsibility for your life. Motivation increases within an expanding mind and mental attitude is altered through a basic shift in thinking. It's a matter of using the resources already within you to attract happiness, success and peace. By doing what stimulates your mind, interesting hobbies can divert attention away from mundane thought by activating the creative parts of the brain. When a person is being creative, they tend to breathe more diaphragmatically and because they are so absorbed in what they are doing, anxiety is reduced through a normalizing of thought.

The artist makes good use of the *trance state* when producing a work of art. Here the subconscious speaks through the hand and brush, conveying impressions upon the canvas so the observer can capture a glimpse of the artist's soul. These impressions have been etched into your psyche over thousands of years and find their expression when you are involved in creative play.

Expression is more than just the product of thought; it is also the fulfilling of man's age-long desire to create what is pleasing to the eye and to God. Early man learned how to project his inner thoughts, emotions and instincts onto the cave wall. His urge to hunt, kill and eat soon found its expression in art. And when he would stare at his artistic creation, the impression made upon his subconscious inspired him to hunt and survive better. With regard to imagination, little has changed in forty thousand years.

Note: *In the case history you are about to read, I refer to my client as "Client A." This is done in order to protect the identity of the person and maintain confidentiality.*

Case History: De-stressing through Guided Imagery

Client A, a thirty-four year old male teacher, came to me suffering with stress, due to managing a very difficult class of final grade primary school children. There was one boy in particular who was making life very difficult for him. Because my client was of a gentle disposition, he was letting this boy walk all over him, putting up with insults on a daily basis and sometimes even physical abuse. The cracks were beginning to show, with sleepless nights now a regular occurance, resulting in poor concentration, chronic fatigue, and a few grey hairs to add to it all. Unable to switch off from work, he was surely becoming what he described in his own words as "a nervous wreck." Something had to be done, and fast. Otherwise he was looking at the possibility of having to find a new job.

During his first session of hypnosis, my client went very deep into relaxation. And I suspect on account of simply allowing himself to let go after so many months of constant stress. Among the many observable signs of relaxation he displayed, the most noticeable was the way in which his face muscles fell into repose, and how the lines on his forehead became practically non-existent.

I had begun the induction with slow, smooth, diaphragmatic breathing, and my client remained unconsciously in control of this deep breathing pattern until the end of the session. (The breath acts as a natural deepener in hypnosis. When it is consciously learned and taken charge of at the beginning of an induction, it then remains diaphragmatic throughout, with the person not having to think about it.)

It was obvious that my client was a shy, quiet man. So without trying to turn him into something he was not, I wanted to give him the confidence he needed to control his class in such a way that they would respect him. I asked him to visualize the classroom through the eyes of a child, observing his behaviors and mannerisms as a teacher, but from a school boy's perspective.

"What do you see?" I asked.

"I see a teacher standing at the top of the classroom reading a book to the class," he replied.

"What does he look like?"

"He's tall and thin, with a bald head that's easy to see, because he slouches forward so much. He's afraid of something and doesn't want to lift his head up to look at the class... They're so loud... They're so bloody loud."

"Who are loud?" I responded.

"That bunch of bloody messers... I wish they'd shut up for a while and stop hounding me."

"Well then tell them to shut up," I said. There was a silent pause for about a minute, and then my client let out a roar:

"Shut up!"

"Tell them again," I said.

"Shut up!" he roared, only this time louder. In the minutes that followed my client released much pent up emotion, and when he was done, I got him to take three very slow, very deep breaths.

"How do you feel now?" I asked.

"Better," he replied.

I asked him to go back to observing through the eyes of a pupil once again. Then I said, "Now I want you to imagine your teacher looking straight at you, and then walking confidently towards you. How does this make you feel as a child sitting down in the class?"

"Worried," he replied.

"Now I want you to rewind the scene and play it back again in your imagination, only this time I want you to be the teacher. Feel what it's like to be confident and in full control of the situation. Inhale and think of the word *calm*. Now exhale slowly and think to yourself, and in full control. Imagine maintaining eye contact with the child before walking over to him and saying in a confident, clear voice, "Get out of my class, and go to the Principal's office."" Remain calm, but authoritative, and look as though you mean business.

My client played out this scene in his imagination three times. Then I spent the remainder of the session implanting suggestions to increase confidence and self-esteem.

A month later my client reported back to me that he was doing great, and could hardly believe the difference just one session of hypnosis had made. But it was really he who had made the difference. Because he had not sabotaged his goal of being confident and in full control, he was able to move forward, getting better and better each time he had to exercise authority. By *pre-empting* his future through *imagery* he was able to remove unrealistic fear and become the product of his imagination and desire. He said that he struggled at times with maintaining eye contact with the more challenging individuals in the class, but he made himself do it all the same, putting up with the discomfort, so that his mind could learn to get over the fear of it. Throughout the day he would prompt his subconscious with simple, present tense suggestions such as *calm and relaxed, cool and confident, I'm in full control, I'm the boss,* and *I say what goes.* At night he was sleeping well, combining controlled breathing with progressive relaxation before going off to sleep, drawing a clear distinction in his mind between *tension* and *relaxation.* Deep, rejuvenating rest always followed. By learning to tap into his subconscious, he was able to transform what was once a nervous wreck into a healthy, happy, confident and focused teacher. Rather than let reality shape him, he was now shaping reality, allowing it to unfold naturally and easily, just as programmed, just as imagined.

Imagination – The Crucial Component

If there is a war between *will* and *imagination,* imagination always wins the day. Using self-hypnotic guided imagery to attract what you desire, makes life unfold the way you want it to. It's just a case of using your active imagination to anticipate how events will play out and how you will perform during them. Now you are shaping reality to suit your needs, rather than just going along with it in the hope that all will go well. Your imagination is as good as the next person's, so don't think that you've a poor imagination, because you don't. It may be just a little under-used and in need of stimulation. Not enough emphasis is placed on imagination and this is because most of the time it's taken for granted. I cannot stress enough the necessity of using your imagination actively, so use it often and with deliberate intent. Self-hypnosis will help you enhance your imagination, possibly the most wonderful and creative aspect of your mind.

"Our purpose in life is to manifest our dreams."
Dr. Joseph E. Keaney

Part 2

Unleashing the Power Within You

*"Allow imagination to make real your unconscious,
unexpressed wish."*
Cathal O'Briain

Chapter 7

Inducing Self-Hypnosis

"Self-hypnosis is simply allowing the process to happen."
Cathal O'Briain

Back to Basics

Now I am going to teach you how to induce self-hypnosis. I will start by showing you a basic induction. Then I will explain in detail how the phases of the induction work in succession. Hypnotic Inductions *No. 1* to *No. 8* are not for recording purposes. They are so you can learn self-hypnosis at its most basic level. Towards the end of the chapter you will be making your first self-hypnotic recording using a *Confidence and Relaxation Script* I've prepared for you. But for the moment, I would like you to memorize one or two of the inductions below and put them into daily practice. In no time you'll have them off by heart. But for now, just get to grips with the basics of your first hypnotic induction.

Induction No. 1: Basic Induction

Concentration Phase

Lie down and fix your eyes at a point upon the ceiling. Exhale completely.

Every time you inhale, count a number down in your mind, beginning with the No. 10.

Take in 10, very slow, very deep breaths (Counting back from 10 to 0) while concentrating at a point upon the ceiling.

Just keep your eyes fixed upon this point while you breathe very deeply.

When you reach the count of 0, close you eyes as you exhale.
Think only of your breath.

Set the Body Clock

Say to your subconscious, "I'm spending 10 minutes in hypnosis today."

Apply Suggestions

You can use the suggestions I have given below or you can make up your own. Here are some examples of precise, present tense suggestions you can give your subconscious. Repeat and imagine each one three times. When implanting suggestion and image remember that, **repetition** increases **retention**. Your images will become you.

"I feel confident, relaxed, and in full control."

(Imagine and involve your senses)

*"With each day that passes, I am getting **stronger** and **stronger**."*

(Emphasize)

Implantation Phase

Now give your mind a little time to digest these suggestions and images. Just let your mind wander for a while. It will do so all by itself. After spending a few soothing minutes in trance, your body clock will automatically remind you that time is up. Now you must draw a conclusion to the hypnotic session by directly informing your subconscious that you wish to terminate the session and become consciously alert. This is how it is done:

Termination

Say these important words to yourself:

"On the count of three, I am fully aware, and fully alert"

*"**1**, I am coming out of hypnosis now"*

*"**2**, I am ready to be fully aware and fully alert"*

*"3, My eyes are open and I'm **fully aware** and **fully alert**, **fully aware** and **fully alert**"*

At this point open your eyes, sit up straight, take a deep breath, and stretch gently.

The above induction is simple to apply once practiced. It is a very effective way to induce trance and I recommend you use it at least three times before moving on to the next induction. That way your subconscious will grow accustomed to trance gradually, helping you achieve a deeper, more relaxing state each time. Now I'll explain in greater detail what exactly is going on in the *basic induction* and how the different phases of the induction work in conjunction with each other during self-hypnosis.

Induction No. 1: Basic Induction (Explained)

The Concentration Phase

The purpose of this phase is to relax your mind by concentrating on two things only, the point on the ceiling and your breath. As you stare and breathe, your conscious mind begins to switch off. In this day-dream state your subconscious naturally comes to the fore to protect you from any presenting dangers that could arise while you are not giving the surrounding environment your full attention. Concentrating on a fixed point helps you to slip into the light trance state (the alpha state), because the conscious part of your mind gets bored of staring, and thinks to itself,

"I'd much rather take a nap now than continue to stare at this point on the ceiling."

Now you are ready to close your eyes and relax deeply. Your conscious mind greatly welcomes the rest and rejuvenation that follows.

Setting the Body Clock

During hypnosis there is a time distortion where twenty minutes may only feel like five minutes and vice-versa. So it's important to set your body clock by suggesting to your mind how long you intend to spend in hypnosis.

Applying Suggestion Phase

The subconscious is very similar to a busy computer. Because it has no ability to reason, the information you program it with must be carefully worded and thought out prior to the induction. When it comes to implanting suggestions, try and remember that you are communicating with a subconscious that takes things very literally. Keep it simple and avoid any ambiguous language that may cause confusion about what it is you desire. Start with suggestions of least importance, followed by suggestions of greater importance, finishing up with suggestions of most importance. Whatever suggestions you decide on, put emotion behind them. *Imagine them, believe them and feel them.*

The Implantation Phase

When a suggestion, image, thought or idea has been given to your subconscious, you must allow it time to be digested and programmed into your mind. You may accomplish this by diverting your attention to another thought or image that is completely unrelated to what you've just finished implanting. At this point in the induction you simply let go. It is where you move from a medium to a deep trance as your mind just wanders off to a pleasant holiday you were on last year. Suggestions are always best implanted in the medium trance state of hypnosis. Because when you allow your mind to go into deep trance, you feel considerable lethargy, both physically and mentally. You may feel as though you do not want to move or even think. Enjoy the experience and let your mind do the work all by itself.

Termination

You can terminate the session by clearly demonstrating to your mind that you wish to finish up. It's not a good idea to just get up and go about your business without terminating the session. Every induction must be brought to an end. By seeing through the termination procedure fully you are drawing a clear distinction in your mind between deep relaxation and normal conscious awareness. If you are tired and want to go asleep, you can bring an end to the session by saying in your mind,

"On the count of 3 my hypnosis session is over, and I am ready to go asleep."

If you happen to fall asleep during hypnosis, that's fine. But during the day I would prefer if you did not use it for going to sleep, as dozing off may become a new learned response, thus making hypnosis counter-productive.

Additional Phases for Your Next Induction

Progressive Relaxation Phase

Progressive relaxation is relaxing the entire body from head to toe through concentration and relaxation. The technique you are about to learn is the most basic one, but can be expanded to include more body parts. As always, the breath is central to its application.

The Progressive Relaxation Technique

Lie down and fix your eyes at a point upon the ceiling.

Breathe slowly, smoothly, silently and completely.

Inhale and clench your left fist tightly.

Feel your arm and shoulder tensing as you breathe in.

Imagine tension moving from your body directly into your fist.

Now exhale and relax your hand, arm and shoulder.

Imagine tension being released from your fist into the air, like steam being released from a pressure cooker.

Do the same with your right fist, arm and shoulder.

Return to your left hand, only now, position it so that your knuckles

are facing the ceiling.

Stretch out your fingers as far as they will go and pull your hand back as if you are waving to someone, keeping your arm glued to the chair or bed.

Feel the tension in your forearms while you inhale and imagine tension moving from your body directly into your stretched out hand.

Now let go of it by relaxing your hand and exhaling deeply.

Do the same with right hand, arm and shoulder.

Inhale and tense your left foot by pointing your toes forward.

Feel your calves, lower and upper leg, thigh and hip tensing while you breathe in.

Now exhale and relax the entire area.

Do the same with right foot and whole leg region.

Return back to your left foot, only instead of pointing them forward, this time pull your toes back towards you while you inhale.

Feel the tension and concentrate on the regions being affected.

Now exhale and relax the entire area.

Do the same with the right foot and then settle into deep relaxation.

The tensing of each body part in alliance with the breath helps the mind and body to distinguish between *tension* and *relaxation*. It takes a little bit of getting used to but the result is complete physical relaxation. The technique is also very useful outside of hypnosis for simply relaxing the body before you go off to sleep. Self-hypnosis is good for overcoming insomnia. If you have difficulty getting off to sleep, use progressive relaxation and then suggest to yourself, *"I am getting tireder and tireder, sleepier and sleepier, and very soon I'll be asleep."*

When you have given your mind these suggestions, divert your attention to something pleasant with no further thought of sleep. It's important not to think about it anymore because thinking and trying only prevents your mind from producing sleep. A pleasant sleep should follow.

The Deepening Phase

The deepening phase is similar to the relaxation phase, only this time you are also giving your subconscious suggestions for deeper relaxation:

*Inhale and say **10** in your mind, exhale and say, **so calm.***
*Inhale and say **9** in your mind, exhale and say, **so relaxed.***
*Inhale and say **8** in your mind, exhale and say, **deeper and deeper.***
*Inhale and say **7** in your mind, exhale and say, **deeper and deeper.***
*Continue saying, **deeper and deeper** with each count down.*
On reaching 0, allow yourself to drift for a while.

The Imagery Phase

The imagery phase is where you imagine a special place, somewhere quiet and peaceful, where you feel completely at ease. It can be fantasy or based on somewhere that really exists. The main thing is to use your imagination, because in hypnosis your imagination is more active and vivid. In this phase you can imagine a beautiful white sandy beach or a lush green forest. What you imagine is up to you. Over time you will know how your special place should look and feel. While you are there, see yourself looking happy and content. Create positive images of perfect health and total relaxation. This is the best place to instill a positive self image.

Now that you know all the various phases of the induction process, let's put them into practice. Just allow the process to happen through belief and expectancy.

Induction No. 2: Basic Induction with Additional Phases

Progressive Relaxation Phase

Relax each and every part of your body in succession the way you have learned.

Concentration Phase

Lie down, fix your eyes at a point upon the ceiling and exhale completely.

Every time you inhale, count a number down in your mind.

Begin with the number 10.

Take in 10 very slow, very deep breaths (counting back from 10 to 0) while concentrating at a point upon the ceiling.

Just keep your eyes fixed upon this point while you breathe very deeply.

When you reach the count of 0, close you eyes as you exhale.

Think only of your breath.

Set the Body Clock

Say to your subconscious, *"I'm spending 20 minutes in hypnosis today."*

Deepening Phase

*Inhale and say **10** in your mind, exhale and say, **deeper and deeper.***

*Inhale and say **9** in your mind, exhale and say, **further and further.***

*Inhale and say **8** in your mind, exhale and say, **deeper and deeper.***

*Inhale and say **7** in your mind, exhale and say, **further and further.***

On reaching 0 allow you mind to drift deeper all by itself.

Imagery Phase

Now imagine that you are walking along a path through a lush green forest. The sky above is blue and there's a fragrance of pine and flowers in the air. You are listening to all the wonderful sounds of nature and there is absolutely nothing for you to do, but simply relax and enjoy this quiet, peaceful walk...

This is an example of the sort of scene you can imagine in this phase. It's in the imaginary phase that your desired self-image can be created and maintained.

Apply Suggestions

Remember: **repetition** increases **retention**. Your images become you.

Finish with suggestions of most importance. Imagine and repeat them three times.

For example:

"I feel confident and full of energy."

(Imagine and repeat)

"I always remember to breathe correctly."

(Imagine and repeat)

Implantation Phase

Now give your mind a little time to digest these suggestions and images. Just let your mind wander for a while.

Termination

Say these important words to yourself:

"On the count of 3, I am fully aware and fully alert."

"1, I am coming out of hypnosis now."

"2, I am ready to be fully aware and fully alert."

"3, My eyes are open. I'm fully aware and fully alert."

Open your eyes, sit up straight, take a deep breath and stretch gently.

At this point in the book you have the choice of learning more inductions or moving on to chapter 6. Most of the hypnotic Inductions are compiled together in this chapter so you can reference them easily. As you read the book, you can keep coming back to this chapter to learn more inductions. That way you can keep refreshing your mind in the basics as you enjoy the rest of the book.

Induction No. 3: Candlelight and Staircase

Note: *please be careful when using a naked flame.*

Concentration Phase

Sit down and fix your eyes upon the flame of a burning candle. Exhale completely.

Countdown 10 deep breaths while staring at the flickering flame.

On completing the breaths say this in your mind:

"My eyelids are getting heavier and heavier... heavier and heavier ... heavier and heavier... heavier and heavier... and the more I try and keep them open, the more they want to close."

Then close your eyes and say, "My eyes are locked tightly together and I am deeply relaxed."

Set the Body Clock
Imagery Phase

Say to your subconscious, *"I'm standing at the top of a beautifully carpeted staircase. Each step down brings me deeper into relaxation."*

Now begin stepping down and saying *deeper and deeper* with each step that you take.

4 – Deeper and deeper. 3 – Dreamier and dreamier. 2 – Further and further.

1 – Deeper and deeper. 0 – Just let yourself go now.

Imagine there is a door in front of you. Say to yourself, *"This door is the entrance to my safe place. When I open this door I'm going to be more deeply relaxed than I've ever been before."*

Open the door and walk into your safe place (beach, forest, mountain, etc). Spend some time in your safe place implanting images of how you want your life to be. Here you must empower your self-image by rendering up bright, colorful pictures in your imagination of a happy and healthy life.

Apply Suggestions

Finish with suggestions of most importance. Imagine and repeat them 3 times.

For example:

"I am sharp, focused and motivated."

"I am full of confidence and I love socializing."

"With each day that passes, my health is getting better and better."

Or whatever image you wish to implant.

Implantation Phase

Allow your mind time to digest these suggestions while you just flow and drift.

Say to your subconscious, *"The next time I hypnotize myself, I go much deeper."*

Termination

Now bring hypnosis to an end by terminating the session the way you know.

Induction No. 4: Rapid Induction

Sit or lie down comfortably.

Find a point in the room to stare at and exhale completely.

*Inhale and say 10. Now exhale and say **relax.***

Do this until you have reached 5 and then close your eyes.

*Continue counting down to 0, saying **deeper and deeper** as you exhale.*

When you have reached 0, let yourself drift off for a while.

Induction No. 5: Fingernail Gazing Method

Sit down on a comfortable chair and start breathing deeply.

Extend your right or left arm out so that your hand is level with your shoulder.

Tilt your hand slightly upward so that you can clearly see your fingernails.

Concentrate intently upon one of your nails and do not take your eyes of it.

Allow a feeling of heavieness and tiredness to come into your arm and your eyes.

As the heavieness begins to pull your arm downwards towards your lap, allow your eyelids to get heavier and heavier.

Now say in your mind, "When my hand touches my lap, my eyes close and I move into hypnosis."

Keep your eyes fixed upon your fingernail. Let your eyeslids get heavier and heavier, while your arm also gets heavier and heavier.

When you feel your hand making contact with your lap, close your eyes and take a deep breath as you move into trance.

Induction No. 6: Elastic Band Resistance Method

Sit down on a comfortable chair and begin breathing deeply.

Imagine there are elastic bands holding your wrists to the arms of the chair.

Start moving your wrists upwards and imagine the elastic beginning to stretch.

Feel the force pulling your wrists down as you try to move them up.

And the more you try and raise each wrist, the tighter the elastic pulls them down.

Allow your wrists to raise up just a few inchs in height, until eventually, you just have give in and let them drop.

When they drop, close your eyes, take a deep breath and move into trance.

Induction No. 7: Eye Blinking Method

Focus your eyes upon a point and begin breathing deeply.

Count back from 20 in your mind, blinking your eyelids once with each count.

As you count back, allow both your counting and your blinking to slow down.

On reaching 0, close your tired eyelids and move into trance.

Creating Your Own Personalized Recordings

Included in this book are hypnotic scripts for your own private use in *self-therapy*. They cover many problems and have been carefully selected from my own personal collection of scripts. They can be recorded on an old tape cassette recorder, or using the latest software on your computer, all depending on the type of recording equipment you have. Here is how to make your very own personalized recording:

Find a room where there is no noise except the sound of hypnotic music playing gently in the background.

You can download hypnotic music from the internet or buy it in good bookstores.

Before recording, take a few deep breaths and relax.

When you are nice and settled, begin speaking slowly, softly and clearly.

Your voice should remain monotone throughout, not going too high or low, and making sure to keep the pace consistent.

Remind yourself to slow down and stay soft toned, almost boring to listen to.

Whenever you see a word or sentence in italic, slow down; these are the deepeners in the script and must be drawn out as you say them.

Whenever you see a comma, pause for a second as you would normally.

Whenever you see (Pause) in brackets like this, take 3 deep breaths and then continue where you left off.

This period of respite will help you to relax while making and listening to the recording.

When you are listening to the script in hypnosis, these periods of quiet will allow your subconscious mind time to digest the material that has been implanted.

At the end of the recording, terminate the session and fade out the music slowly.

Here is an example of a paragraph from a typical script, similar to the type of script you'll be using from now on. Take your time saying it, and watch out for the pauses:

So as you begin to walk again, along the path, and down the garden, you find that you are drifting deeper, deeper and deeper, deeper and deeper (Pause). The smell of fresh flowers in the air, the rich vibrant colors that surround you, the sound of the wind blowing gently through the trees, all envelop your senses now, with wonderful feelings of peace, and calm, and the more you breathe, the more your relax, and the more you relax, the better you feel (Pause). So calm, so quiet now...

Hypnotic Deepeners

At the beginning of each script you will be using a deepener. Below there are three different types of deepener which you can vary between and use. The three deepeners can be put together to make one big one if that is your wish. The idea is to pick a deepener you like or create your own one and apply it to the beginning of the script you have chosen.

Deepener No. 1: Creating Heavy and Floating Sensations

Concentrate your attention upon a point and take 5, very slow, very deep breaths, inhaling the calm, exhaling the tension, inhaling the calm, exhaling the tension (Pause and give enough time for breaths to be taken). And again, I'd like you to take 5, very slow, very deep breaths, inhaling the calm, exhaling the tension (Pause). And now, your eyelids are beginning to get heavier, and heavier. And the more you try to keep them open, the more they want to close, because now, they are heavy, so very, very heavy, so just close them down now, all the way, down, down, relaxing deeper, and deeper. And with every breath that you take from now on, you're going to find yourself, drifting deeper, and deeper. For surrounding you, is peace, and comfort, quietness, and stillness, and nothing is needed from you, and nothing, is expected of you. And with every breath that you take, it's a nice feeling, a nice, relaxed feeling, while you just float and drift, drift and float, softly and gently, like a feather on the breeze, drifting and floating, floating higher, and higher, softly and gently, like a feather on the breeze, drifting and floating, floating higher, and higher (Pause).

Once you have finished the deepener, you can begin your chosen script.

Deepener No. 2: Counting Yourself Down

And now, I'd like you, just to allow your eyes to gently close, just allow your eyes to gently close, and listen, to the sound of my voice, your subconscious mind, now becoming more receptive to the words that I am saying to you (Pause). And now, I want you to take 3, very slow, very deep breaths (Pause). And with every breath that you take from now on, you're going to find yourself, drifting deeper, and deeper (Pause). And now, I'm going to count you slowly down from 3 to 0, and as I count you slowly down, from 3 to 0, with each count that I make, and with every breath that you take, you're going to find yourself, drifting deeper, and deeper. And by the time I have reached the count of 0, you are going to be more deeply relaxed, than you have ever been before.

3 You are getting sleepier, and sleepier, dreamier, and dreamier, sleepier and sleepier, dreamier, and dreamier.

2 And you, are beginning to feel heavier; your body, is beginning to feel heavier, and heavier. Your arms and legs, feel so heavy now, so very, very heavy.

1 Almost down now, into complete and total relaxation. Sinking down, down, deeper, and deeper, down, down, deeper and deeper.

0 Right down now. You are more deeply relaxed than ever before. So calm, so quiet now. Feeling inside you, a wave of relaxation, moving from the top of your head, all the way to the tips of your toes (Pause).

Once you have finished the deepener, you can begin your chosen script.

Deepener No. 3: Progressive Relaxation

I want you to think about the top of your head, just think of your scalp, where all that tension begins, and allow those tiny little nerves and muscles in your scalp, to become relaxed now, so very, very relaxed. And just imagine that relaxation, moving from your scalp, down into your forehead, and just feel the lines on your forehead smoothening out, going loose, limp, and relaxed (Pause). And just feel that relaxation, moving down into your cheeks, and into your jaw, and just allow your teeth, to fully unclench, and let your jaw relax, and sag (Pause). And just imagine that wonderful feeling of warm, blue calm, spreading down into your neck, and into your shoulders, and just allow your neck muscles, and your shoulders, to go limp, and relaxed (Pause). Think about your arms, the bone, the muscle, the blood, circulating freely, your elbows, and your forearms, so beautifully relaxed, and resting, perfectly at ease. Think about your chest, and your back, relaxing, and resting. Imagine at the top of your spine. There is a ball of white, healing energy there. I want you now, just to feel this white ball of energy, moving down through your spine, soothing you within, relaxing you, and healing you, moving down, down, down through your spine, making its way to the very base (Pause). And from the base of your spine, just imagine the healing light spreading out to your hips, and now to your thighs, moving down through your legs, and into your knees, relaxation, spreading into your calves and into your heels, feet, and toes. From the tips of your toes, all the way to the top of your head, every nerve, every muscle, every sinew, is now relaxing, and resting, as you allow your mind, to drift deeper, and deeper, deeper, and deeper. And now, I'd like you, just to take 1, very slow, very deep breath (Pause).

Note: When making your personalized recording I would like you to incorporate some background music into the session. But before you do I want to explain why I feel music is so important to self-hypnosis.

Music – Food for the Soul

Music has the ability to alter mood dramatically, while its healing qualities seek nothing more than our desire to listen. While the pace and rhythm changes, so do we, following its direction as it leads. Consciously we stop thinking. Unconsciously we start feeling, as the settling inside comes about naturally and easily. Inspirational therapy and motivational science interact with each other as sound passes through the ear, vibrating miniature bones to gain momentum on its way to the unconscious listener. People who involve themselves in music experience greater focused attention, increased imagery, positive feelings and heightened awareness. By allowing ourselves to become involved in what's known as the flow experience, subjective changes can be made on a physical, perceptual and cognitive level. This is why music has a therapeutic role to play in self-hypnosis, and is why we call it *food for the soul*.

Although I want you to use music in your daily hypnotic inductions, if you would prefer to relax without music, that's perfectly fine. There's a lot to be said for silence. As you well know, it's golden. Personally I find background music greatly enhances the hypnotic experience. If you choose it wisely, you will find it very complementary to your trance sessions. I'd like to mention that it's important you don't become dependant on having music as a necessity for relaxing. If your subconscious comes to believe that it's a necessary tool that you can't perform self-hypnosis without, you may find it harder to relax when there's none around. Just see it as another part of the overall experience and enjoy the way it helps you to relax as it naturally increases your endorphin level.

The human brain is divided into two hemispheres. The right side is identified as the seat of musical appreciation, even though listening to music involves two-sided activity. Both language and music use both sides of the brain but not completely in the same way. When we are using music in self-hypnosis our aim is to keep conscious activity low while promoting subconscious activity to a higher level. So avoid music with rapid changes of frequency and intensity. Use gentle, continuous and uncomplicated music that encourages right-sided activity, keeping the breath in the foreground and music quietly in the background.

There is a wide variety of hypnotic music available on the internet, in music shops and bookstores. Finding what best suits you comes down to personal choice. I recommend that you change the background music each month to give your mind some variety. When choosing music to listen to outside of hypnosis, be aware that music can create sickness. Because it has such a powerful effect on the psyche, inappropriate music can be bad for health. So choose wisely because its effects on us are instant and long lasting.

Recording the Script

I would like the script you are about to record to become your main and most used script. It's for relaxing and instilling a positive self-image. But it can also be used in helping a wide range of emotional problems such as fear or anxiety. Feel free to customize it to suit your particular needs, and remember to take your time and enjoy making it.

Confidence and Relaxation Script

(Use one of the deepeners from this chapter at the beginning of the script.)

And now, I want you to use your imagination. I want you to imagine, that you are walking along a straight path, through a lush green forest. The sky above is blue, and there's a wonderful smell of pine, and flowers in the air. You are listening to all the sounds of nature, and there is absolutely nothing for you to do, but to enjoy this calm, quiet walk through the forest. And here in this part of the woods, nobody wants anything from you, and nobody expects anything from you. There is absolutely nothing for you to do, but to relax, and enjoy. And as you walk, you take in the surrounding beauty, a beauty that envelops your senses, with wonderful feelings of peace and calm. It feels as though you are completely at one with yourself, as you allow your mind to drift deeper, and deeper, deeper, and deeper (Pause). The old, negative thoughts you once had, have now been left behind in the past, for good, as you walk happily and assuredly along the straight path, where the warm sun gently filters through the trees, and touches off your skin. And while you move calmly and gently, you now realize that you are feeling better, better than you have felt in a long time. You feel as though you are completely free. Free to be happy, and free to move on from anything that does not make you happy. Maybe in the past you wondered if you were ever going to feel completely free. Well now you are, and from this moment on, you remain that way. This realization is now in your heart, is now in your mind, and is now in your soul (Pause). And now the child within you is beginning to surface and wonder, and daydream like you once did as a child. And like a child, you now simply observe all the beauty that surrounds you. And while you look and listen, relaxing perfectly and completely, you notice how easy it is to breathe the fresh pure air into your lungs. Now you are completely in control of your breathing. You are breathing calmly, gently, smoothly and easily. And the more you breathe, the more you relax, and the more you relax, the better you feel. And the more you breathe, the more you relax, and the more you relax, the better you feel. Relaxing deeper, and deeper still, just letting go, completely (Pause). Further off in the distance, you notice the figure of a person walking towards you, and as they draw closer, you begin to make out who this person is (Pause) it's you. The person walking towards you (Pause) is you. And as you draw closer to yourself, you can't help but notice how well you are looking. You are dressed in your finest clothes, and you are smiling, like you've never seen yourself smile before. There's a glow of happiness on your face and a confident stride in your walk, and you look as though you haven't a care in the world. After a short time, you are eventually standing face to face with your ideal self, and without giving it a second thought you say,

"How are you? You're looking great today."

Almost in the same instant, your ideal self opens their arms wide, and gives you a hug like you never experienced before. It's a hug straight from the heart, and it embraces you with strength, and unconditional love. The hug is so powerful, it causes your ideal self to pass straight into you, and become you. Your ideal self (Pause) becomes you, and you are now the person that you've always dreamed of being. Your fantasy has become reality, and you are now very pleased with how the new you looks and feels. It's as though you've made peace with yourself, and as though a new you has been created along this wonderful journey. Going deeper, and deeper now, deeper, and deeper, just letting go, completely, relaxing more, and more, deeper, and deeper. So as you begin to walk again, along the path and through the forest, you become aware of the sounds of nature all around you. Birds are singing away to their hearts content, and you are happy just to stop and listen to their song. And while you continue walking, you hear the sound of a nearby stream and turn off the forest path to go in search of it. Your instinct guides you to where it is flowing gently, and so you sit on a log beside it, to have a well earned rest. And while you sit and listen, to the calm, lapping sounds of the water, a thirst comes over you, and you realize that you are very thirsty, from all the walking you've done, and so you kneel down, and cup your hand in the stream, for a nice refreshing drink of cool, pure, fresh water. And when the water touches off your dry lips, it feels cool and pure, and so you drink, and satisfy your thirst. And when you are finished drinking, you notice a reflection in the water, and you see yourself in the reflection. You realize that the person you are looking at is someone you are very proud to be, and so you take some time to stare and smile at your reflection, because the person you are smiling at (Pause) is you, a confident, and relaxed person. Life is good, and is now very exciting for you, because now you are allowing your subconscious mind to express your growing confidence. You accept yourself, and love yourself, and all the wonderful changes that are occurring inside you, changes that you are aware of, and other changes, which are now happening at a deeper level. You realize that every learning experience is like a stepping stone to greater success and freedom. Every day you program happy thoughts and positive thoughts into your mind. You are smiling more and laughing more, expressing yourself freely, because now you are motivated, and deeply relaxed. You are optimistic about your future, and are confident in your ability, to accept, and successfully handle all challenges that come your way. Each day you encourage yourself with positive thoughts such as, "I can do it. I am doing it. I'm full of life and I'm full of energy. I'm confident. I'm relaxed. I'm creative. I'm motivated. I'm healthy. I've a healthy mind and I've a healthy body."

You trust yourself to be poised and serene, calm and confident, as you express your ideas in a clear and logical way. Others enjoy your company, and look forward to hearing your ideas, because you always express yourself in a clear and logical way. You have confidence entering a room, confidence in your appearance, and confidence in your personality. You are always relaxed and confident, because you now know the great depth of your own inner strength.

Chapter 8

Goal-Setting through Self-Hypnosis

"Man is a goal seeking animal. His life only has meaning if he is reaching out and striving for his goals."
Aristotle

About Goal-Setting

It's a well known fact that people who set goals tend to achieve more positive results in their lives than people who don't. Directing your life towards achieving meaningful goals often results in greater peace of mind. People often set goals, only to discover after a short time that they can't reach them. This can happen when you do not fully understand how *goal-setting* works. It also happens when you are not too sure about what you really want or need out of life. A person may want to lose weight, which seems like a worthy goal. But somebody else may want an expensive car when they don't actually need one. Something we must consider is that setting goals is not the entire answer to success. It's the action you take in realizing your goals that creates real success. The only way to achieve a goal is to first have a true intention of doing so. The action that follows then becomes the true measure of your intention.

When choosing a goal you must consider the effect it will have on all aspects of your life, family, career, health and inner happiness. It's about being realistic and prioritizing the things that are truly important to you. Ask yourself an important question: *is the goal attainable?* A goal is attainable when it's feasible in relation to your resources. By this I mean, if your goal is to become a professional golfer within three years, but you have neither the money, the time, nor the physical ability to train, then your goal is unattainable. This is why you must come up with a strategy that makes sense. You must consider factors in relation to your age and financial position when choosing one. Goal-setting in self-hypnosis is cheap, simple and very enjoyable. Implanting goals in your subconscious is a goal in itself. One that is both challenging and attainable, providing of course you set aside some time for it each day.

Goal-setting in self-hypnosis will give you the edge over others who use regular, conscious methods of attaining goals. Hypnosis will enable you to reinforce your desired objectives through the full use of your powerful subconscious mind. Typical goal-setting is a conscious activity, which by its critical nature can encourage sabotaging behavior. Once you implant your desired goal, by using auto-suggestion and imagination regularly, it will be much harder for your conscious mind to foil your plans and dreams. The deeper part of your mind loves positive change. So once you clarify your truest intentions and communicate them clearly to the subconscious, the process of helping you achieve goals then becomes irreversible within your new subconscious program.

Setting a Deadline

Set a deadline for when you want to achieve your goals. Unlike other day-to-day activities that don't require deadlines, goals do. You will need to know when you are going to get there. So by working within a time frame, you can remain focused, motivated, and dedicated. If you don't reach your goal by a set deadline, this does not mean you have failed. It simply means that you need to extend the time span for reaching your desired target. If your goal depends on an event rather than a date, determine what event must take place first; and then do whatever is possible to make that event happen. For example, if your goal is to get rid of excess weight within three months after you quit smoking then set a date to quit smoking and take appropriate action to quit smoking. If the event is something beyond your control, such as working towards a goal after a family reunion, then have a backup plan in case the reunion gets cancelled or postponed.

Goal-Set For You Alone

When you are setting goals, I want you to set them for you. There's a natural tendency to include the ones you love in all your dreams. This is understandable. But going in on a goal with someone else only makes it harder to achieve in the long run. When the other isn't pulling their weight, this only acts as a disincentive to continue the joint agreement. Too many dreams have been broken by one person wanting to go all the way, and the other pulling out halfway. If you want to have a share in someone else's dream, support them on their journey. With a bit of luck, they will do the same for you. When life goals are your own and you do not achieve them, then you only have yourself to blame.

How to Goal-Set Using Self-Hypnosis

Goal-setting in self-hypnosis will take you anywhere you want to go with your life. In a heightened state of awareness your efforts are more concentrated and directed. They are also without the distraction of mental interference. By setting and reaching challenging but realistic goals in the present; you create a stepping stone that brings you closer to achieving your important life goals. Often people dream and fantasize about what they want, but fail to create a plan of action that's within their capacity. By clearly planning short term goals to be achieved in the present, you are then in a better position to reach them on a daily basis. This helps your long term goal to move ever closer. Now I'll show you how to goal-set in self-hypnosis.

Relax into the hypnotic state using one of the inductions in chapter five.

In the Imagery Phase, see the goal as if it has already been accomplished.

Imagine your personal benefits for achieving your desired goal, including your emotional satisfaction and attitude of gratitude for these benefits.

Imagine the process you have to go through in order to achieve your goal.

Visualize clearly and colorfully what life will be like once you've achieved it.

In the Apply Suggestion Phase, imagine and repeat suggestions three times for achieving your goals, for example:

"I find it easy to focus on my goals."

"I am strong, determined, and very proud of myself."

"I am accomplishing all my goals."

"I am reaching my daily targets with ease."

Life Goals

Life goals are large overall goals to be accomplished within a lifetime. They are the product of your truest intentions, and contain your greatest ambitions. You must choose your life goal wisely. You don't want to discover after years of dedication that what you thought was good for you, just wasn't right for you. When you decide on a life goal, you must realize that your entire world is going to revolve around it. A relationship between you and your goal will develop and build. From time to time things may come between you and your life goal; but by regularly using self-hypnosis, you will find you have the necessary tools for achieving success. Your breath, suggestion and imagination will help guide you on the path towards a better, more fulfilled life. But you must remember to command your subconscious at every available opportunity. It's there to help, serve and protect you.

Some people look at television and watch others happily achieving their life goals. It often inspires the one who is watching to say "I could do that!" But they should really ask themselves the question, "Is that what I really want?"

So many people start new ventures they haven't given much thought to, only to discover way down the line that it really wasn't for them. Take as much time as you need before deciding on a life goal. You'll be glad you did when you see it coming to fruition.

When you decide on a life goal, set a deadline as follows:

Break it down into yearly goals to be achieved. A life goal that takes five years to reach is broken into five yearly goals, the yearly goal into twelve monthly goals, the monthly goal into four weekly goals, and the weekly goal into seven daily goals. Then each day you do whatever it takes to achieve your daily goals.

Creating and Implanting Your Daily Plan

Creating a daily plan on paper is the correct way to goal-set. You should do it prior to self-hypnosis. This is how it is done:

Make out a list of attainable goals and memorize them for self-hypnosis.

Implant your goals in hypnosis that morning to be carried out the same day.

Alternatively, you can implant goals in the evening to be carried out the following day.

In the evening review your daily plan by crossing off the goals you've achieved.

Tick the ones you have not achieved.

Sometimes a simple thing like bad weather can stop us from reaching our daily goals.

If you can't manage to fulfill a goal for whatever reason, just stick it on your daily plan for the next day.

When making a daily plan, the important things to remember are:

Make a list of goals that you can achieve in one day and be specific.

Make sure they are realistic, attainable and challenging.
Underline the goal you consider a priority.

Rewarding Your Goals

Give yourself credit where credit is due. Each day as you complete your goals, give yourself time in hypnosis to thank your subconscious for helping you achieve them. If a close friend helped you reach a goal, you would thank them from the bottom of your heart. Well your subconscious is your best friend, so don't forget to thank it.

Goals are dreams waiting to be realized. The interest that is generated from pursuing a goal keeps the mind active and alive. Psychological and emotional illness is far less likely to occur in a person who is committed to fulfilling their goals. One can even learn to eliminate an existing condition if the desire to reach a goal is strong enough. Goal-setting helps you move forward by merit of what you've already achieved. It is this very act of moving forward that makes goal-setting so desirable to your subconscious. And is why goal-setting must become an integral part of your self-hypnotic sessions.

Below is a goal-setting script you can record. It will empower your subconscious with the ability to set and achieve those important goals in your life. Feel free to insert your own personal words to enhance it. Use precise, present tense suggestion. It will spur your imagination to render up vibrant images of you achieving your goals. *Imagine it, experience it, believe it!*

Note: *When reading the script aloud, remember to pause for a second where you see a comma like this(,). Whenever you see the word* pause *in brackets like this (Pause), take in three, very slow, very deep breaths.*

Goal Setting Script

(Use one of the deepeners from Chapter 5 at the beginning of this script)
As you continue relaxing, become aware of how powerful

your subconscious is, and the way in which it makes changes occur, directing energy inside your mind, finding new solutions, while it moves you ever closer to your aspirations, your dreams, and your goals. Realize that your subconscious has the capability, the skill. And so it's just a matter of utilizing these wonderful talents you already possess. For you are determined, focused, and deeply, deeply relaxed, so deeply, deeply relaxed (Pause). And the more you plan, the more you achieve, and the more you achieve, the further you go. Going further and further, deeper and deeper, further and further, deeper and deeper (Pause).

The quality of your life is improving in every way. Your feelings of confidence, security, and peace are also increasing steadily. And as you grow stronger within yourself, with each day that passes, your daily goals become more challenging, your objectives more stimulating, and your imagination more active, visualizing your dreams and goals, with bright, colorful images, with you at the center of this action, calm, relaxed, and in full control, breathing regularly, and deeply, regularly, and deeply. And the more you breathe, the more you relax, and the more you relax, the better you feel. And the more you breathe, the more you relax, and the more you relax, the better you feel. And with every breath that you take, you're going to find yourself, drifting deeper and deeper, deeper and deeper, down, down, down, all the way now (Pause for 2 minutes). You realize that as you relax, your ability to focus and concentrate is enhanced. And now you are becoming more aware of your freedom to go beyond the limits, to push yourself that extra bit further, and really go the distance. The goals you set out to achieve make you go the extra distance, they put you to the test, but that is your choice, to be put to the test, for if it was simple, you would not learn anything new about yourself. And the more you prepare, the more you succeed, and the more you succeed, the further you go. And the more you prepare, the more you succeed, and the more you succeed, the further you go. Going further and further, deeper, and deeper, further and further, deeper and deeper (Pause). Your goals and dreams depict the real you. Allow these words to sink deeply now while you just drift for a while. Drifting deeper and deeper... (Fade out)

Chapter 9

Habitual Behavior and Emotional Disorders

"Obsessive thinking and compulsive behavior are partly fed through negative, destructive, self-punishing language. Language can be a curse unconsciously."
Cathal O'Briain

Understanding Obsessive Thinking and Compulsive Behavior

Compulsions are basically mental or physical behaviors that a person repeats in order to bring about relief from anxiety. With compulsive behavior, the mind conforms to strict rules relating to the individual's *obsession* or *ritual*. *Stability* replaces *distress* once the compulsion is *given in to*. This feeling of elation is usually at complete opposites with the chaos and disorder that is felt by the individual shortly before the compulsive act is carried out.

This regaining of control must follow rigid guidelines and be nothing short of perfect. The sufferer may know well that their thoughts and actions are indeed excessive, or that they are totally unconnected to what it is they are trying to neutralize. Every time the action is repeated, the obsession gains momentum and unconscious value. Obsession and compulsion are known to accelerate quickly in times of emotional stress.

Compulsions are *physical rituals*. Obsessions are *psychological rituals*. But the compulsion is of much greater value to the sufferer than the obsession, for it's the most easily accessed point of relief from obsessive thoughts. Simple, repetitive acts can provide pleasure and gratification at a deep level. With little regard for logic, there is a strong desire to participate in the ritualistic behavior, despite feeling embarrassed. Obsession draws a person inwards through self-punishing language. Although it may feel satisfying to give in to a compulsion, the energy of the mind is still nonetheless consumed through fearful self-inspection. Over time this type of negative introspection can give rise to mental illness and serious emotional problems. The person in the midst of a serious obsession may stop looking externally for happiness. They can become distant from people and life itself as they engage too much in the ritual. Even the most stable people are prone to habitual behavior, especially in times of increased stress. The subconscious may protect, maintain or enhance an obsession in order to detract your attention away from the real issues in need of address. Unresolved problems can create and amplify compulsive behavior. So if you want to put an end to obsession, you must reveal the real source of your anxiety. This is best done by seeing a professional *Analytical Hypnotherapist* who is qualified and trained in *Hypno-Analysis*. Their job is to get to the *root cause* of the obsession. But this should only be done after seeing a professional healthcare practitioner.

Because *Obsessive Compulsive Disorder* is an anxiety disorder, it must be treated as such. Finding out its root cause through analysis with a qualified therapist is advised, because not all *OCD* is solely habitual. It is sometimes related to trauma in memory, or to an unhappy childhood. Performing certain rituals may be a way to keep certain repressed thoughts and impulses away from consciousness.

Rituals are both satisfying and humiliating, but essentially are meaningless. They serve to bolster the obsession, which in turn commands the compulsion. How we break this vicious cycle is by using hypnosis each and every time it feels as though a ritual must be performed.

For example, rather than wash your hands a second time, sit

down and focus your attention upon a point in the room. Begin deep, controlled, diaphragmatic breathing. Think only of your breath and allow your eyelids to get heavy. Then close your eyes gently and think of the last holiday you were on. Involve the senses. Bring up all the good feelings you normally associate with being on holidays. Now say to yourself, *"I'm in full control."* Render up an image of you in full control and with your hands in your pockets. Make this image big, bright and colorful. Keep breathing very deeply and allow for those crucial moments of respite between the breaths. Now give your self a *post-hypnotic suggestion* such as, *"The sound of running water reminds me to breathe very deeply and relax."* or *"The sound of running water reminds me to protect the environment by washing my hands only once."*

Now you can terminate the session feeling proud that you did not give in to obsession by acting on it. In others words, you got through the moment. Getting through the moment is vital for re-training your mind to overcome obsession. There is nothing to fear by not giving in to what an obsession demands of you.

Recognizing Obsessive Compulsive Behavior

Obsessions are recurrent, persistent thoughts, images or impulses that present themselves within an obsession. These intrusive thoughts are not typical worries about real life problems. If not repressed, they are neutralized instead through repeated action; this is what makes them compulsive. Here are a few examples of OCD behavior:

Washings hands a number of times because they do not feel clean enough.

Counting the same numbers over and over again, or repeating words.

Becoming pre-occupied with pulling your hair out or biting nails.

Reacting aggressively when you have the ability to remain calm.

Avoiding cracks in the pavement when walking.

Excessive drinking when you know that it's killing you.

Locking the door three times or switching the light on and off repeatedly.

Ways to Help Overcome OCD

Stop the obsession by making a decision to end the ritual.

Focus on a date in hypnosis.

On this day you will end the ritual and replace it with deep breathing or whatever your preferred substitute is.

By ending the ritual, you help end the obsession.

You must put up with a certain amount of discomfort in order to overcome an obsession.

Get through the moment knowing that the feeling of anxiety you experience cannot harm you in any way and will shortly dissipate.

By ignoring the ritual and getting through the obsessive period without acting out the usual repeated actions, your subconscious takes one step closer to freedom.

Remember the predominant emotion behind an obsessive thought is fear.

The compulsive action is a symbolic way to avoid the fear; but this is unnecessary when danger is not imminent.

Your subconscious has the power to overcome unrealistic fear, but you must first believe that there is actually nothing to fear at all.

Trying not to think about an obsessive thought will only result in stronger obsessive thoughts; so allow your thinking free reign, but do not give in to the compulsion.

This will result in temporary anxiety, but is the best way to end the obsession.

Obsessive traits are common in most people, but if you suffering symptoms as a result of obsessive behaviour, seek professional help.

Left out of control, OCD can lead to more serious mental and physical problems.

With permission from your therapist, this book can be used as a complement to professional treatment.

"By not giving in to the compulsion, you help to end the obsession."
Cathal O'Briain

Emotional Disorders

An *emotional disorder* could be defined as: *any mental disorder not caused by detectable abnormalities of the brain, where there is a major disturbance of emotions.* When we refer to *emotional disorders* we refer to *psychological disorders* that affect *emotion;* for example, *anxiety* or *depression.*

Post Traumatic Stress Disorder (PTSD) is an example of how the effect of trauma plays a significant role in altering the emotional and psychological make-up of a person. PTSD not only involves the victim, but tends to have an adverse effect upon their family and friends too. Strong emotional forces project themselves outwardly when triggered, often making the sufferer irrational and unpredictable. Recurrent recollections, external cues, disturbing dreams, all can make life very hard for someone with PTSD. A person recovering from *trauma* may avoid people, conversations and stimuli that remind them of what's happened. This is natural and understandable, but when a person hides from the fact that something bad has happened to them, by simply trying to ignore or forget it, this is when emotion can take on a new and more destructive form. PTSD is serious and must be treated by a healthcare professional.

With emotional disorders, action must be taken inside the subconscious. It is the seat of your *primary emotions*, where your *core feelings* are accessed and revived. Core feelings are instinctively driven and spontaneously surface in the body in the form of motivation and drive. *Emotion* is the motivating power of the mind. The reason we do what we feel, is because our core feelings are driving us. But when they are not present, we tend to rely on our *secondary emotions*. An example of this would be feeling disappointed when your core feeling is anger. If anger does not express itself, this emotion can turn into anxiety. The real difference between a primary emotion and a secondary emotion is that primary emotions tend to come and go, spurring you into action when you are connected to your core feelings. But secondary emotions tend to feel more constant and with no real significant driving force. Trauma has the ability to disconnect a person from their primary emotions, leaving them more reliant on their secondary ones. Left to their own devices, anxiety and unrealistic fear have the power to move a person from normal worry into serious depression.

Depression

Depression could be described as *a state of intense sadness and despair that has advanced to the point where it is affecting the personal, family and social life of the individual.* Depression can be mild, moderate or severe in intensity. Many people with depression don't seek treatment. This is usually because they simply don't recognize their illness as being treatable. Depression is treatable and should not be ignored. Set-backs in life such as financial loss, marital problems, and illness, all can give rise to depressive symptoms such as sadness, fatigue, and a general lack of interest. Depression can be overcome, but first the sufferer must regain control with professional help.

Many people experience reactive depression at some point in their lives. A death in the family or losing a job can be enough to set up the precondition for disappointment to become reactionary in the future. During a bout of reactive depression, a person can be irritable and preoccupied by what's happened to them. But this dull mood usually lifts as they begin to recover. It is probably the most common type of depression.

Endogenous (unipolar) depression is when depression has its origins in the psyche. If an unpleasant life experience is responsible, it is most likely to have happened some time in the past. Endogenous depression can be *chemical* or *biological* in make-up as well as *psychological* and *emotional*. *Fatigue* can be an early symptom, with the individual frequently waking at intervals throughout the night. They may feel very low in the morning, finding even the most simplest of tasks impossible to do. This can make life very difficult for the sufferer; the depression is coming from within and is being nurtured and kept alive by the current program running in the subconscious.

Bipolar depression is a mood disorder that is characterized by the alternations of *manic* and *depressive states*. Its symptoms include those of *endogenous depression*. But there are also periods of mania during which the depression can create feelings of elation in the mind and body. This mania or elation, although pleasurable to experience, can be detrimental to health. Biological susceptibility to inheriting depression can be one cause. But additional factors like marital and work-related stresses must always also be considered. A person with no family history of bipolar may develop it, beginning perhaps with a reactive episode, followed by more episodes, until eventually the person has become both manic and depressive. People with very low self-esteem can be prone to this type of depression. Self-hypnosis is very effective in treating bipolar depression, but professional help must be sought first. This is most important!

Dysthymia is a mood disorder characterized by mild to moderate depression with symptoms of sadness, despair, engulfment, pessimism and loss of appetite. It typically develops in early adulthood and is more common in adult women. Often there is no obvious cause; but its symptoms can be brought on by anxiety, stress, illness, substance abuse, etc. It has the genetic ability to run in families, but is not as severe as other types of depression. Dysthymia as an emotional disorder is paradoxical in nature. Although its symptoms are relatively mild on a daily basis, over a lifetime of endurance they take their toll on the body.

Ways to Help Overcome Depression (In Alliance with Professional Help)

Consult a healthcare professional and get to the root cause of your depression.

Know that you have the necessary skills and resources to overcome it.

Be willing to change what you are presently doing.

Stay in control of your breathing. Spot-check it regularly.

Breathe with positive suggestion as much as possible.

Make time to implant vivid images of change, in self-hypnosis.

Implant positive suggestions and healthy self-images throughout the day.

Think of depression as something you've already overcome.

Look after your diet. Drink plenty of water and eat well.

Keep your mind interested and divert attention to what is external.

Take up a hobby if you don't already have one.

Get into the fresh air as often as possible. Cut down on television.

If you notice that you are feeling sorry for yourself, Stop!

Set challenging, realistic goals to be achieved on a daily basis.

Postpone stressful decision making until your head feels clear.

Be on your guard for sabotage. It's one of the main reasons people don't recover from depression. By acknowledging it when it rises, you overtake it.

One step forward and two steps back is just a concept that doesn't apply to real life.

If you feel as though you are doing well and then experience a setback, remember that here you have a choice. You can revert back to old ways or you can simply return to the peace you were enjoying before the setback occurred.

Make sure you laugh at yourself from time to time. This takes the edge out of depression and helps you to overcome fear.

Phobias

A *phobia,* from the Greek meaning to *fear* or *dread* something, is a persistent abnormal response to particular situations, stimuli or persons. There is usually an excessive and unreasonable desire to avoid the feared object. Phobias are the most common form of *anxiety disorders.* They involve persistent, intense anxiety responses to specific feared stimuli. Because of this, a person with a phobia will either go out of their way to avoid a situation, or endure it with great difficulty.

Specific phobias relate to specific objects and are the most common type of phobia. The majority of specific phobias don't cause any real problem. This is because when a feared entity is not present, it doesn't produce a *phobic reaction.* An example of this would be a business woman with a fear of pigs living in the city. As long as the object of her fear is not in the immediate environment, she can live without the phobia interfering with her daily routine. But other phobias such as *agoraphobia* and *claustrophobia* can make life very difficult, especially when daily activities involve some level of contact with what is dreaded. Some specific phobias, such as a fear of certain types of people can begin early in life. These phobias usually dissipate with maturity and social contact. Other phobias, such as a fear of insects, heights or flying, often develop later on in life. *Social phobias* can cause high levels of anxiety in social and public situations. Sometimes they can develop from an effort to make sense of a feeling of panic: The person assumes that because they feel anxiety they must be afraid of something, and so a new object or situation becomes a new phobia.

Gradual exposure to a feared object or situation is a good way to train your imagination to desensitize the phobic environments that cause you anxiety. Using suggestion and imagination is another useful way to combat phobias. Here are some examples:

Fear of Flying

Phobic suggestion: *I hate flying. I don't feel safe in the air.*

Positive suggestion: *I enjoy flying. I feel completely safe in the air.*

Social Phobia

Phobic suggestion: *I wonder what everyone will think of me.*

Positive suggestion: *I love going out with friends. I look and feel great.*

Agoraphobia

Phobic suggestion: *I need to get out of this place before I collapse.*

Positive suggestion: *I'm safe and secure. I'm in full control.*

Needle Phobia

Needle phobia or *Belonephobia* is basically a fear of sharp objects such as needles or pins. Even minor procedures such as taking a blood sample can create quite a strong resistance in a person. From what I've observed in my own clients, this fear of needles can eventually develop into a stronger fear, not only of needles, but also of objects or situations associated with needles. Examples of these would be syringes, dental equipment, blood, band-aids, medicinal creams, white coats, or even the smell of hospitals. The phobia is often caused by traumatic childhood events, but may also be the result of over-reactive parents or family members in the presence of sharp objects. It affects many people, often to the extent that it causes the sufferer to avoid seeking medical care and attention. Those with needle phobia tend to stay clear of the medical profession altogether. This is the biggest problem that faces its large population of sufferers.

Science has also shown us that needle phobia has a genetic component. It's a genetic trait that once had a survival value for mankind. Many of our ancestors were continually introduced to dirty, infectious needles prior to the twentieth century. So in an effort to remain infection free, we naturally tend to avoid needles.

Our unconscious has been programmed to believe they are a threat, more than a cure. This is why people naturally tend to fear needles.

Gradual Exposure

It's common for young children to be afraid of needles, but in time most outgrow their fear. Other children become adult *needle-phobics*. Some children have an acute sensitivity to pain; so needle procedures that are painless for one child can cause considerable pain and trauma in the needle-phobic child.

When dealing with a needle-phobic child, parents can use positive reinforcement. For example, if the child is distracted by a toy and doesn't make a fuss, this should be reinforced by saying, *"Now that was easy, wasn't it."*

And the next time your child gets an injection remind them of their previous success by saying, *"Remember the last time you were here? It was easy, wasn't it."*

Rewarding your child is a good way of strengthening positive reinforcement. Gradual exposure to needles can help a child overcome their phobia. If you let your child watch another child who is comfortable with receiving an injection, a kind of buddy system is put in place. Now the comfortable child can support the fearful child. This is a very useful way of changing a child's attitude to needles.

An important step in gaining freedom from needle phobia and phobias in general, is the re-education of your belief system. This is done by rooting out misinformation and replacing it with truth. This can be done effectively using self-hypnosis. Regaining self-control is done by learning how to relax around feared objects, people and situations. By reintroducing yourself slowly to the feared object through imagery in self-hypnosis, you can inform your subconscious that there is actually nothing to fear. By studying and concentrating on the needle within your mind, you can gradually expose yourself to its harmlessness, thus reducing its fearful effects in the present. A person doesn't need to be able to touch the sharp end of the needle to prove to themselves that they are over a phobia. To a degree, the sharp end is meant to be feared, because it's sharp; but not to the extent where it has become a phobia.

Anxiety

Anxiety is a complex emotional state often backed up by unpleasant mental and physical sensations. These sensations can include chest pain, headache, high blood pressure, digestive and immune dysfunction, sweating, trembling, nausea, pupil dilation, difficulty concentrating, worry, sadness, persistent fear, apprehension, insomnia, a need to go to the toilet regularly, along with many other symptoms. Anxiety has *cognitive, emotional* and *behavioral* components, but is still nonetheless a common emotion like *fear*. It can be *acute* (short term), or *chronic* (long term). Cognitively, the brain readies the body to deal with what it perceives as a threat to survival; pupils dilate, blood flows to the major muscle groups and the person begins to sweat, powering up in an attempt to cope with a threat that often doesn't exist. Emotionally, anxiety can create a feeling of panic and unrealistic fear in order to move you away from a perilous situation. Behaviorally, the body gears up to face the threat by means of nervous and muscular stimulation. These functions of the mind and body are there to help you deal with anxiety by either fighting or running away from the source of it (fight of flight). This kind of anxiety is a normal response to fear and stress and helps you to manage testing situations. But when anxiety starts to take over and control your daily experience, this is when action must be taken to reduce it.

Generalized Anxiety Disorder

Generalized Anxiety Disorder (GAD) is where anxiety is felt consistently and very often without recognizable cause. It's as though fear has spread itself thinly throughout the body, overwhelmingly at times, but nearly always constant. GAD is where anxiety is more in control of the person than they are of it, causing emotional and psychological problems, fears and phobias.

State anxiety is another form of anxiety and is when a person reacts to a particular environment, situation or stimuli. It is similar to a conditioned reflex and is common in most of us. You can reduce state anxiety by pre-empting upcoming events through active imagination (process and result imagery), or by breathing with positive suggestion throughout a stressful occasion. From time to time the subconscious will try and stop you from doing something if it has not been reassured that everything will be okay. This is where you must exercise suggestive control so that anxiety can be minimized or removed completely.

"I am calm, relaxed and in full control," is a clear instruction to the subconscious that control has been accomplished. This very suggestion spurs the imagination to render up an image of someone who is in full control and anxiety free. Now the subconscious can dutifully set about making this image of control into reality.

Reducing Anxiety through Sustained Trance

The next time you feel a little anxious at home, find yourself a chair or a bed and then settle yourself down. Locate a point on the ceiling and take ten deep breaths while you concentrate on it. Take another 10 deep breaths only this time saying *calm and relaxed* while you inhale and exhale deeply. While you are counting, allow your eyelids to get heavy. As they get heavy, try and keep them open... But the more you try, the harder it becomes to stop them closing... until eventually... they close, right on completion of your 20th breath. Now you have moved into trance, so just allow your breathing to normalize. Let your mind drift and every once in a while just say to yourself *deeper and deeper.* This will help you to sustain or deepen the trance. Now the mind is getting a nice relaxing treatment, where it can regenerate and build up energy to look after your mind and body.

Self-hypnosis is not just about implanting suggestion; it is also about basic relaxation. Stillness of mind can be enjoyed over lengthy periods of time if that is your wish. It's really about whether or not you have the time. An hour in trance will keep your head clear and body anxiety free.

Case History 2: Anxiety

Client B, a forty-three year old woman, came to me with emotional problems. Her complaint was that she was suffering from severe anxiety. She told me that up until the previous year her marraige was harmonious, but then came into difficulty all of a sudden and for no obvious reason. She described how her character was literally transformed overnight, from a wife and mother who was kind and caring, into someone who was angry and unpredictable. An overwhelming fear had consumed her, with panic attacks occuring regularly, and difficulty getting to sleep. She had little or no appetite and was steadily losing weight, much to the concern of her family and friends. However, her main worry was the current dissconnection from her husband, created in her own words by "an inability to relate to anyone or anything."

Over the course of therapy we explored many of her memories, particularly those of early childhood. There were several accounts of being left alone for hours on end by parents running a busy farm. Schooling was strict, as was home life, with discipline and punishment laid down by her father on a daily basis, that was sometimes violent. One sound that kept surfacing in her mind during her recollections was of her father's hand striking her leg. She also remembered looking in the mirror at the track of his hand across her face, and the hot, pulsating feeling it created on her skin.

She released much pent up anger in her first two sessions of analysis, directed mostly at her parents. Then in session seven, she recalled two memories of being abused by an uncle at around the age of five. Throughout her life she had always felt as if something bad had happened to her, but had no observable memory of these disturbing events.

As these memories surfaced, I got her to explore them in as much detail as possible. By viewing these past events in hypnosis, a considerable weight was lifted from her mind and body. How she achieved this was by expressing herself verbally, as if her uncle was standing right in front of her listening. Finally, she was letting go of many years of pent up hurt, emotion, anger, guilt, disgust and shame. Then there was silence, marking the beginning of her recovery. By getting to the root cause of her anxiety, she was able to observe and accept the past, where as a mature adult she was now in a better position to reason with what had happened to her.

Finding the courage to forgive was the most difficult part of the healing process for my client. But by the end of her analysis, all parties were forgiven, including her uncle.

This case history is an example of how a team effort between therapist and client can yield positive results. It also illustrates how self-therapy used in conjunction with ongoing analysis can increase recovery time. Even when you lift repression and negative emotion, it doesn't necessarily mean a swift recovery will follow. The reason my client recovered so well was because she changed her way of thinking. In other words, she changed her subconscious attitude. Getting to the *root cause* of her anxiety revealed the force driving her behaviour. Once she overcame this force, she knew it was then up to her to look after her own mental and physical health through self-hypnosis.

Panic

A panic attack may leave a person feeling completely exhausted.

This fatigue is caused by the excessive amounts of adrenaline being released every time a panic attack is under way. Once adrenaline makes its way into the bloodstream, it travels to the areas of the body that can get you quickly to safety, such as the major muscle groups. When adrenaline is in full flow, digestion is put on hold so that the brain can become entirely focused on fighting or fleeing. Attacks can last anything up to an hour, or can be as short as just a few seconds. A negative reaction to an external stimulus (similar to state anxiety, or a conditioned reflex) encourages a vicious cycle to begin, with *fear breeding symptom,* and *symptom breeding fear.*

Agoraphobia is a condition where there is a fear of not being able to escape from a situation. Anxiety that is not equal in proportion to what is actually being faced fills the bodily system in an almost trigger-like response. Overwhelming fear then plays its part in getting the person away from the situation as quickly as possible. This dread can sometimes be accompanied by a surreal feeling of time distortion, or a sense of non-reality. With most panic attacks, the physical source is nearly always the same. It is an inappropriate response of the *amygdala* (a part of the brain that regulates emotions and triggers response to danger).

A panic attack must be nipped in the bud before it escalates. Attention must be diverted away from what is causing panic through distraction and relaxation. A good way to distract your mind is to focus in on your breath. This can prevent *hyperventi-lation* from making the panic attack worse. Hyperventilation is when you breathe faster than is necessary for the given situation. By exhaling slowly and completely through pursed lips, you increase the relaxation response and decrease the fight or flight response. When breathing in through your nose, fill your lungs gently and without making a sound. If you breathe in too fast and forcefully, you only increase the *arousal response.* So breathe in quietly, and breathe out very, very slowly.

A person with heartburn could lead themselves to believe that they were in the first stages of a heart attack; but the one who just passes it off as heartburn does not create the precondition for fear to set in. The suggestion *"I'm having a heart attack,"* has the instantaneous ability to establish a strong connection between fear and symptom. So long as the person focuses on the symptom, the link between fear and symptom is maintained. One must divert their attention to a point outside of themselves to sever the connection between fear in the mind and symptom in the body.

A panic attack will run its course if not stopped in its tracks. But if anything, panic is more of a *cardio-workout* for the body than an actual life-threatening experience. The fear of having another panic attack is often brought on by the first one. The fear of what's to come is what begins the cycle. One attack reinforces the next, until eventually they become an almost daily experience, with no catalyst even required to bring one on. How you reduce fear and prevent the cycle beginning in the first place, is by making it clear to your subconscious that panic attacks are not life-threatening. The foundation for a future panic attack is laid down before it's experienced; so invest time and energy anticipating a healthy future rather that pre-empting what you fear through imagination. A panic attack fuels and manifests itself. By taking away the fuel that ignites a panic attack, which is fear, you eliminate the possibility of having another one. Although the sensations experienced during a panic attack can be very unpleasant, scientific evidence has shown that these sensations cannot harm you. The real problem with having them is the level of anxiety reached every time you encounter one.

Panic attacks are common but this doesn't mean they should be tolerated. You must seek out their cause. This can be done with the help of a healthcare professional trained in the area. A certified hypnotherapist can regress a person to the time of the symptoms' original appearance using *hyper-amnesia* (a type of age-regression where details of memory become enhanced). Using a method known as *free association*, the client is encouraged to allow one memory after another to pop into consciousness while in hypnosis. During the course of analysis the unconscious mind grows accustomed to passing up memory for rationalization. This then prepares the individual to deal with and desensitize repression as it appears in consciousness. Hidden memories, guilty thoughts, suppressed beliefs, and traumatizing experiences all have the ability to create anxiety, panic, and other emotional disorders. Their conscious realization means that they are no longer outside of the person's control, but instead have new symbolic meaning through reasoning and reconciliation. Overcoming panic requires you to locate and employ your natural resources. It is you against panic, and you must win. The same organs that create panic also reduce it, so trust and believe that you're going to be fine and that you are always in full control.

Chapter 10

Natural Energy Enhancement

"The energy of the mind is the essence of Life."
Aristotle

The Energy Within

When I say the *energy within,* I refer to the internal life-force created by your breath, use of suggestion and imagination, an instinct drive, a powerful libido, a sense of fear and through a basic need to survive. The things that generate energy in your mind and body are natural. None of them require additional energy boosters in the form of pills, drugs, stimulants, remedies or energy drinks. These are just profit-making products that advertisers brainwash people into thinking they need. These so-called energy stimulants were of little use to prehistoric man when the need for food required him to spend days on end walking in search of his next meal. Even if they were around, he would have gladly exchanged them with someone for the fat on their chop.

Unfortunately we live in a fast moving world. Because it has us so preoccupied with making money, people sometimes forget that they have their own natural resources for creating energy. We seek out quick-solution, artificial energy-makers to enhance our alertness levels. And it seems the more we spend on these products, the greater the illusion becomes; that somehow the new pill we consume will get us through our hectic day better than the last one did. If you believe that some power drink has given you a lift, it is probably because you suggested to your mind "This drink will give me energy."

This positive suggestion alone may provide enough information to bring about an increase in energy. It's really a question
of what works well in persuading your belief system. If one of
these power drinks claims to *boost* your body and mind, the
advertising label *boost* may well be enough to make you feel as
though you are getting a boost. If the same product said *exhaust*,
a rapid decrease in energy would almost certainly be noticed
shortly after its consumption. The truth behind most energy
drinks is that they are loaded with caffeine, leaving you feeling
anxious and more drained than you felt before you drank them.

There's a lot to be said for the common A to Z vitamin,
mineral, herb and cod liver oil capsule. If you take them on a
daily basis, continue to do so; they are all good for maintaining a
healthy body. Their natural ingredients help us to stay active; but
overloading your system with sugar or caffeine to create energy
is just an unnecessary waste of money. It is also bad for your
health. If you enjoy the taste of coffee, drink it for that reason but
don't go drinking three cups of it in the morning just to give your
body a kick. It is a proven fact of science that caffeine in large
quantities is dangerous. So if you are a coffee addict and wish to
get your caffeine intake under control, there are a few herbal
coffees on the market that contain no caffeine or acidity.
Decaffeinated coffee is a better alternative to regular coffee; but
it's important to remember that it still contains a small amount of
caffeine. It's also usually higher in acidity due to the type of bean
that's used for enhancing flavor after the decaffeinating process.
Withdrawal from caffeine can be hard on the health; so I
recommend cutting down gradually before eventually switching
to herbal coffee and tea only.

The energy within is completely natural and likes us to use
natural ways of enhancing it. You wouldn't give a child a cup of
coffee if he or she seemed to be lacking in energy. Nor would you
feed a greyhound on a diet ginseng pills to make it run faster.
Well, the same should apply to you. By increasing energy the

natural way, we may increase and sustain it by the most powerful force on earth: *Mother Nature*.

In self-hypnosis you automatically build up the energy within by allowing your mind and body to relax and recuperate. After moving into the hypnotic state, you can use your imagination to render up powerful images of action. *Action* speaks louder than *words*. By presenting a strong picture of action to the mind, the subconscious can go about increasing energy in order to make real whatever you imagine. Visualizing yourself playing your favorite sport for three or four minutes is a good way of presenting an image of action to your mind. Part of your subconscious mind's function is to direct energy. When you implant images of action, you can then repeat energy-promoting suggestions such as, *"I'm full of energy."* or *"Energy is flowing through every part of me, like a bright light rushing through my veins."*

By communicating to your subconscious with simple, concise language, that is both desirable and believable, you will almost certainly feel an increase in your energy within a short period of time.

In self-hypnosis you can give your mind a post-hypnotic suggestion to be carried out in the future, for example:

"It's Saturday the fourteenth, the day of my important football match. I am fit, focused, and full of energy."

Post-hypnotic suggestions to be realized in the future are then repeated and reinforced in further sessions approaching the important date. If your goal is to win the match on Saturday, a good way to help reach that objective is to use process imagery and result imagery.

"Where the focus goes, the energy flows."
Dr. Joseph E. Keaney

Process Imagery for Energy Enhancement

Process imagery is where you visualize yourself in preparation, training hard and going through the motions needed to win and achieve success. Often people lose the edge and notice a significant drop in energy approaching big events. Process energy helps gives you the edge, because when the big day finally arrives, you know that you are truly prepared.

Simply imagine the process, experience the process, maintain it and you will build on your energy. Now it's just a matter of realizing the result already implanted. If you imagine the end result repeatedly, the mind by its very nature must and will do everything in its power to make real these images.

Result Imagery for Energy Enhancement

Result imagery is where you visualize the successful completion of your goal as if it's already achieved. Here you imagine yourself receiving the trophy and being congratulated on your win at the end of a perfect match. This allows the subconscious to clearly see your future reality. With a vision of the end result, your subconscious can make the physical and mental changes necessary for you to bring the repeated images into reality. You then keep your energy at the maximum level until the desired conclusion is accomplished. By combining process and result imagery, you can use them for anything you wish to endeavor, from playing chess to treating ill-health.

Remember to keep suggestions positive and in the present tense. Avoid using negative future tense suggestions like, *"On Saturday I won't be lacking in energy."*

If even remembered, this vague suggestion to be carried out in the future will only give rise to the mind dutifully responding in a negative motor action. In other words, it will help you lack in energy on the day in question. The total of our life's experiences to date are recorded in the *now*, therefore future suggestions are also recorded in the *now*. By using the present tense, you are already there, full of energy and winning.

A lack of energy is not unusual. It is something that everyone experiences at different times throughout the day. The key to enhancing energy is to keep your mind interested, excited and focused on what it is you are engaged in. You must create a desire to unlock energy. The more you lose yourself in a hobby or interest, the more energy you naturally create. Getting the right amount of rest, food, and exercise are equally as important.

Avoiding Stress to Conserve Energy

Another way to increase energy is to avoid stress. The human body is naturally programmed to react to stress from a survival point of view, by moving the person's energy from their body into their brain. This internal programming enables us to focus completely on the choice of either fighting or running away from the source of anxiety. The problem is that many people nowadays are under constant low levels of stress, but their bodies are still reacting to it as though it were life-threatening.

I know that stress can be hard to avoid at times, but a good way to start is by spending less time with people who drain the energy out of you. The reason why you sometimes feel so tired after talking to certain people is because they are masters at listening to the sound of their own voice. Through need, demand and selfishness, they find ways to suck on your energy to bolster up their own. All too often it happens because we allow them to. Those who listen and allow conversation to have its turn keep energy flowing equally. In a group situation you can sometimes observe one person seeking to dominate the group conversation by feeding off everyone else's energy. As more people listen to them, they become louder and more domineering; this is how some people enhance their energy levels. And although it's good to possess strong leadership skills, it isn't fair on others around you not to allow a word in edgeways. When you listen to others and they listen to you, all parties can benefit from the energy being transported backwards and forwards. So bear this in mind the next time a friend needs a shoulder to cry on. Although they might genuinely need you to listen to their troubles, it may also be true that they have a history of using your compassionate nature to bolster up their own energy. By the end of the meeting they feel refreshed, but you feel drained. This is because the flow of energy went only one way, from you to them.

Reflect on both the past and present, and notice how you sometimes get a sudden surge of energy when involved in a pleasurable activity. Then notice how it just seems to deplete when faced with the prospect of doing something you don't want to do. The energy you need is already within you, but your subconscious may need a little persuasion before passing it up to you. The reason it sometimes must be convinced that you need energy is because it may be thinking that it would rather be somewhere else more comfortable, like in bed dreaming. Energy enhancement is mind over matter. Regardless of how tired you feel, you can completely reverse this by spending a few minutes in self-hypnosis.

Ways to Enhance the Energy Within

Create a desire for what you are doing.
Breathe with positive suggestion.
Eat fruit and vegetables (Preferably raw).
Avoid stress.
Get into a natural, healthy environment.

Energy Through Nature

There are a few outdoor places where I like to relax and practice self-hypnosis. My favorite spot is located just a few minutes from where I live. It's a river bank where trees and wild bushes surround me, providing shelter if it rains. No matter what the weather is like, I always make it my business to go there at least once a day. To be honest, I prefer it when it's raining, because that usually means having the riverbank all to myself. In this quiet and tranquil location, large rocks burst out of the river. When the rushing water makes contact with them, it creates a wonderful sound. So while I sit and listen, breathing regularly and deeply, I begin focusing my attention on two things: first, on my breath; and then I focus at a single point on the river. When I'm sure I feel deeply relaxed, I begin breathing with positive suggestion. Now I move into a light state of trance with my eyes open. The sound of the river gets clearer; smell and color becomes richer. The rushing water appears to slow down as my five senses shed a new light on how I perceive things. By joining my index finger to my thumb on each hand, I create what's known as an anchor. Then I say to myself, *"Safe place."*

By creating an anchor and saying, *"Safe place,"* at the same time, I am now giving my subconscious a direct signal to understand that this anchor represents the good feelings I associate with being at the river. This means that when I'm at home using self-hypnosis, by creating the same anchor with my hands, I can automatically bring up the images and good feelings I associate with the river.

The natural environment has an abundance of energy, especially where there are trees and greenery to be found. When you admire the beauty of nature through the senses, it gives off an energy that the body absorbs. The way you maximize this energy is by opening your eyes in appreciation of what surrounds you. This is done through deep breathing and concentrated attention. For those who live hectic lifestyles and work busy office jobs in the city, it can sometimes be hard to find time during the week to go for a nice walk in the hills, or spend an hour or two in the local park. After a while, noise, traffic, concrete buildings and a general lack of scenery all take their toll on your energy. If you work or live in the city, or both, make it your business to get to the local park whenever you can, or take a trip down to the country at weekends. It will do your energy levels the world of good.

Suggestions for Increasing Energy (Breathing with Positive Suggestion)

(Inhale) **Full of life,**	*(Exhale)* **full of energy.**
(Inhale) **Alive,**	*(Exhale)* **and energized.**
(Inhale) **Willing,**	*(Exhale)* **and able.**
(Inhale) **Full of power,**	*(Exhale)* **approaching the hour.**

Note: *The following script for enhancing energy incorporates imagery of a beach. If you would prefer the mountains, a meadow and/or a lake or stream, feel free to edit the script with your chosen imagery. The concept is more important than the specific place you choose. Just make sure your chosen place is a pleasant and peaceful one.*

Energy Enhancement Script

(Use one of the deepeners from Chapter 5 at the beginning of this script)

Once again, go deep inside yourself, to that very part of you that creates energy. And know that every time you do this work, you are giving positive direction to your subconscious; direction that enhances energy, energy that is already inside you, just waiting to be unleashed. So tune in now, and feel this energy deep within your subconscious mind. Give yourself permission to fill up with energy and motivation. And with every breath that you take, the energy in your mind, is now spreading out to the rest of your body, rippling out from your mind, sending waves of energy through each and every cell of your body. From the top of your head, all the way down to the soles of your feet, rippling out gently, carressing every fibre of your being. And in your minds eye, see yourself running, running in your barefeet along a white sandy beach. Feel the sand under your toes, the warm, salty breeze blowing on your skin, while you run with an abundance of energy on your barefeet (Pause for 1 minute). And the more you run, the more energy you feel, and the more energy you feel, the faster you go, running faster and faster, relaxing deeper and deeper, running faster and faster, relaxing deeper and deeper. And while you relax now, become aware of the vibration eminating from your body. This vibration in your body has a source, and that source is your subconscious mind. It is creating the vibration in your body because it is relaxed, and interested, motivated, sharp, focused, completely at ease, intelligent, activated, full of life, full of power. A power that is eminating, vibrating, pulsating, rich in colour, and filled with light, beautiful, colourful bright light. Your mind and body is now filled with a beautiful, bright light, and you are full to capacity, with your very own healing power. The power to move, walk, run, climb, to get up and go out, to see more of the world, and the life you are blessed with. Allow you mind and soul to create vibrations, instilling in you happiness, peace, and prosperity. And the energy you give, give wisely. And the energy you receive, receive graciously (Pause). You are positive, kind and compassionate, and this is what makes you vibrant, and this is what makes you shine. You understand the importance of using your breath, suggestion, and imagination to create energy, all the while you breathe deeply, and easily, relaxing perfectly, and completely. Just allow these important words to sink into your subconscious. Words that fill you with peace, contentment, life and energy.

Chapter 11

Memory, Recall, Forgetting, Repressing and Forgiving

"Memory is all that you were, influencing all that you are."
Cathal O'Briain

Memory Improvement and Recollection

Time and time again you hear people say "I've a poor memory," or "I can't remember anything these days." One thing you should never tell yourself is that you have a poor memory. Always suggest to your subconscious, "I have an excellent memory," or "I find it easy to remember."

By telling yourself you have a good memory, while also practicing some simple memorizing techniques, you will notice a vast improvement in retention. You may also find it easier to move information from your short-term memory into your long-term memory, permanently.

Your brain receives both internal and external information and stores it in short-term memory. If you want to retain something, the secret is to move it from short-term into long-term memory, so that you can retain it for longer than a few minutes. Normally with memory retention, you lose much of the information you take in after just five minutes. Two thirds of it vanishes after an hour. After a day, almost all of it fades through forgetting. You can reverse the process of forgetting; but first you must have a desire to remember. With a desire to remember, you can store information in your long-term memory by using a simple recall technique involving your senses. The more senses you involve in retaining something, the better your memory of it becomes. For example, if you want to memorize a paragraph for a speech:

> *First write or type it.*
> *Then say it out loud while you read it (involve your senses).*
> *Now imagine what you've read as clearly as possible in your mind's eye.*

By involving the senses, while being focused on what it is you wish to remember, you turn the process of *forgetting* into *remembering*. The more you recall something, the quicker you help that information move from short-term into long-term memory. This next technique will help you memorize and recall. It's all you will ever need to have an excellent memory, besides telling yourself and others, "I've an excellent memory."

The Recall Technique
> *Take in the information.*
> *After 5 minutes recall and revise what you are remembering.*
> *After 1 hour do the same.*
> *After 3 hours, do the same.*
> *After 6 hours, do the same.*
> *Recall it once again before you go to sleep.*
> *On the second and third day, recall it 3 times to your memory.*

You now have this information stored in your long-term memory, forever. **Repetition** increases **retention** and is vital for improving memory. Practice the above technique in its entirety. After a few weeks it will amaze you to discover how easy it is to access large amounts of memorized information. I now suggest that you memorize these next few suggestions using the recall technique. Be sure to involve your senses and imagination when using the recall technique.

"My subconscious is extremely capable. It is very adaptive because it learns quickly."

"My memory is excellent. I find it easy to memorize words, thoughts and images."

Forgetting and Repressing

Forgetting is a natural occurrence and happens when the mind fails to retain a memory or impression. It also happens when your mind deliberately creates a *psychological block*. This is known as *repression*. It comes about when you have a motive for not remembering information you wish to *hide* from yourself. It also happens when you give your subconscious a command to *forget it*. These memories, although lost to conscious recall, are never truly forgotten. Your mind just hides them away to protect you, but their content remains, lying somewhere between subconscious and deeper unconscious thought.

An event that feels too traumatic to remain in normal conscious thought is automatically and deliberately passed down to deeper thought where it can remain hidden from consciousness. Although hidden, it still poses a threat to mental and physical health. Memories of a painful nature significantly affect the mind and body in the form of symptoms. When left repressed and unexpressed, their content has the ability to be relived over and over again in the subconscious, eventually causing trauma in the mind.

Symptoms often appear to keep anxiety in check. If removed without first seeking out their *root cause* (for example, repression in the memory), they can result in the individual taking on a new and possibly worse set of symptoms. Every symptom has a cause, which in turn creates an effect. So by getting to the root cause of a problem, you remove its effect in the present. Analytical Hypnotherapy achieves this goal, because the therapist works directly with the subconscious, where the root causes of symptoms have their origin.

Letting Go of Past Hurt Through Forgiveness

Forgiving others for past hurts is easier said than done. But when you forgive, it helps you to let go of the emotion attached to memory. To not forgive is to suffer for what others have done. By refusing to forgive, you remain the victim, because it keeps you locked in the struggle, a kind of prisoner to your own past. It's fair to say that you may never forget certain wrongs done against you, but you can choose to forgive.

Forgiveness benefits you and not the other. As life goes on, from time to time you will recall the hurt and may even have to forgive it again and again. But over time the vividness of these memories will fade, because through forgiveness they cannot remain where the perpetrator owns you. Forgiveness is not an act of surrender, but rather it is a desire not to hold resentment in the act of self-interest. Holding anger and resentment against those who have hurt you by not forgiving them, means you are bound to them by an emotional link. When you forgive, the link is broken and you are free. Mahatma Gandhi once said "The weak can never forgive. Forgiveness is the attribute of the strong."

Ending Self Punishment Through Self-Forgiveness

Sometimes we are more forgiving of strangers than we are of ourselves. Making mistakes is a part of life. When you don't see a mistake as something to learn from, it can be perceived in the mind as something for which you must be punished. In the past you may have sinned in your own eyes, but instead of forgiving yourself, you may have deliberately repressed it. In hiding this memory that made you feel guilty or ashamed, your mind was probably doing what it thought was right for you at the time. But in trying to forget it, all you actually accomplished was to allow punishment to happen at a deeper level. When punishment happens at a deep level, it produces symptoms.

There are times when you even have to forgive yourself for

things you have not done. In the earlier stages of life, sensitive children direct blame inward for the actions of others. So now you must also learn to forgive yourself for holding onto this self-blame for so long. What others do to us is often the cause of our own self-punishment. What you really need is less self-punishment and more self-forgiveness. If you find it hard to forgive yourself, start by forgiving yourself for not being a good forgiver. This in itself is forgiveness, and you have already taken the first step. The self-forgiving person is not a selfish person simply because they chose to let go of self-punishment. On the contrary, the one who remains unforgiving in their world of self-doubt and persecution is more likely to lead a selfish life. Self-forgiveness stops us from constantly internalizing with critical judgment and helps us to keep moving forward.

If an individual hurts you in some way, you have a risk of harboring thoughts of hate towards that person. Such thoughts are natural and understandable, but should not be left to grow inside. In the end, these thoughts will only leave you feeling angry and guilty. This is because they make you feel that you are bad for having a desire to hate or even harm the perpetrator. Here you have a choice: you can go on hating and feeling resentment towards this person, allowing them to destroy your self-image; or you can forgive yourself for having such thoughts, thus letting go of them completely. If you choose the latter, then the memory of them hurting you, as well as the emotion of you hating them, will no longer have substance through resentment; instead they will find release through forgiveness.

Induction No. 8: Releasing and Forgiving

Note: *This exercise will help you forgive and release if you can allow every suggestion to work for you. If you experience any difficulty in letting go of past hurts after several attempts, then seek out a competent hypnotherapist to assist you in this important process.*

Concentration Phase

Lie down and fix your eyes at a point on the ceiling.

Take 10 deep breaths while staring at the point on the ceiling.

*Take 10 more deep breaths only this time incorporating the suggestion, **calm and relaxed**, while you breathe with positive suggestion.*

When you have completed the breaths, close your eyes.

Deepening Phase

*Inhale and say **10** in your mind. Exhale and say, **so calm.***

*Inhale and say **9** in your mind. Exhale and say, **so relaxed.***

*Inhale and say **8** in your mind. Exhale and say, **deeper and deeper.***

*Inhale and say **7** in your mind. Exhale and say, **deeper and deeper.***

*Until the count of **0** continue saying, **deeper and deeper.***

*On reaching **0** say, **I am more deeply relaxed than ever before.***

Imagery Phase

Recall to mind the memory of an event that caused you hurt.

Dissociate yourself by becoming like an older brother or sister to child self.

As an observer, say to your inner-child *"I'm here to help you through this."*

As if watching a play, view it in as much detail from the beginning to end.

If you feel emotion, allow it surface (talk, cry, release it).

If there are guilty parties concerned, causing you hurt, let them know how you feel as an older and wiser observer about what is happening to your younger self.

When you are done expressing yourself, say to them *"I forgive you."*

Now forgive yourself for holding onto the memory for so long.

Say to your inner-child, *"I am always here for you, to protect and take care of you."*

Apply Suggestions
"I have forgiven them."
"I have forgiven myself."
"I give myself permission to release and let go of this memory."

Implantation Phase
Just let go for a while and allow your mind to drift deeper into hypnosis. Allow the important suggestions and images you have instilled in your mind to be digested and programmed into you.

Termination
Bring an end to the session as you have learned. Then sit up and take a deep breath.

Letting go of past hurts by forgiving ourselves and others requires courage, patience and sometimes a little bit more. Only you can measure the depth of your pain; or how long it's going to take you to heal. The hurt attached to memory often remains long after the first experience of the original event. Self-hypnosis helps you to minimize the effects of trauma by strengthening the bond between your conscious and subconscious mind. The past is stored in the present. When you imagine something, whether a future desire or the memory of a past event, the subconscious reacts as though it is in the present. In other words, remembering past events often makes us react as though the event is happening all over again in the present. Because of this, it is in the present where you must heal the past.

"Forgiveness is the fragrance the violet sheds on the heel that has crushed it."
Mark Twain

Chapter 12

Quitting Smoking and Overcoming Addiction

"Stopping smoking is easy. I have done it a thousand times."
Mark Twain

Understanding Addiction and Dependency

No one has ever said that giving up a habit or an addiction was easy for them. In fact, it's a massive achievement to kick a habit and do it right. It takes courage, determination, willpower and imagination to triumph over your demons. But take reassurance in the knowledge that you already have the necessary skills and resources within you to overcome addiction, permanently. Self-hypnosis takes the harshness out of giving up by presenting to your subconscious, alternatives and substitutes that can either equal or replace the old unwanted behaviors. By transferring attention away from the habit, towards healthy meaningful goals, within a short space of time new substitutes become just as longed for as old addictions once were.

An addiction fulfils a particular need or set of needs that cannot otherwise be fulfilled through non-addictive means. Some people have the strength to fight addiction head on (cold turkey) and they are to be admired for their courage. But in order to quit an addiction permanently, without the suffering that's normally associated with giving up, you must first consider the value of your addiction and what it means to you personally. Ask yourself this question:

"What particular need is my addiction trying to fulfill?"

If an appropriate substitution is to be put in place, it must be one that is capable of satisfying your unconscious need for satisfaction as good as the old addiction once did. This is why you must choose your new substitute wisely. It must be equal or greater in value to the addiction you are giving up.

For those with addictive personalities, negative addictions can be turned into positive ones. This is done by increasing your subconscious motivation; where you consistently direct it towards healthy substitutions each day. In the cases of smoking, alcohol or drug addictions, what is needed to put an end to them is a final decision to stop: period. The reason that many people struggle when fighting addiction is because they haven't yet truly come to the point where they are ready to stop their habit. The desire to give up simply isn't strong enough. Consciously they may want to stop, but unconsciously they may not. Without a strong desire to end addiction, you are fighting a losing battle.

To free the mind and body of addiction, you must break away from the environments that trigger your addictive responses. You must deny yourself the luxury of relaxation through addictive means; for example, pondering life after drinking eight pints of beer, or going into a chemically induced trance while under the influence of drugs. Alcohol and drug addiction sucks the life out of personality by stunting the process of maturation. Getting drunk or high regularly as a way to unwind is illogical and dangerous. The last thing that you really do is unwind. How can a person relax knowing they've just blown all their cash on drink or drugs? But that's the least of their worries. Their habit is more than likely ruining their life because they are in the midst of a crisis. Addiction happens easily and mercilessly. It feeds itself in a manner that cares little for the individual, but only for the addiction. If you are suffering because of addiction, there is plenty of help out there. Enjoy using this book as an aid to your recovery. But if your problem is impeding on your life, please get some professional assistance now.

Substance abuse must be combated in a soldier-like fashion if you are to be successful in eliminating addiction. Even for those people with a good ability to stay on top of things, addiction can prove a dominant force at the best of times. This is because at the best of times we tend to celebrate and feed our addictions even more. They are there when you are happy and they are there when you are sad. But if the means to feed the addiction is not present in a time of distress, or if you resort to another, equally damaging substitute, then you can safely say you're addicted. If you truly want to put an end to addiction, you must be willing to make sacrifices. Then you must make a life changing decision – *a decision to **stop**: period.*

The smoker who wishes to give up must visualize him/herself as a non-smoker, living a smoke-free lifestyle. He/she must learn what triggers the response to light up.

'Does a cigarette keep my anxiety in check, or is it just to relieve boredom?'

'What needs am I trying to fulfill by smoking?'

These types of question help you choose substitutions that can equally gratify your pleasure seeking instincts. It enables your habitual mind to unlearn old habits. The reason that alcohol and drugs are so hard to give up is because when they are not present, problems can seem to get bigger instead of smaller. The benefits of the addiction may appear to far outweigh the benefits of giving it up. This is what keeps you stuck, even if your will to give up is strong. You must imagine yourself free.

Addiction is not something you cannot escape from. Addiction is simply a drive that has become habitual through reinforcement. If repetition is responsible, then the addiction must be given a taste of its own medicine in self-hypnosis. Here the suggestion, image and belief that you are no longer addicted can be implanted daily. So too can images of the new substitute that is replacing the addiction. Once the subconscious has established a new way to satisfy its longing for pleasure, it will no longer be happy with just a quick fix, which is all that an addiction can provide.

How to Stop Addiction and Dependency

Instill a real desire to end your addiction using hypnosis.

Doing it for family and friends is not enough.

You must want it badly, and be willing to make sacrifices.

Stop the dependency by making a decision to end the addiction.

Evaluate the possible alternatives and substitutes available to you.

Find the ones that have the capacity to fulfill your needs. This is very important.

Set a date for when you will give up and focus on that date intently, both in and out of trance. Remember; goals are dreams with deadlines.

Pre-empt how your future is going to look by imagining big, bright, colorful images of an addiction-free lifestyle. Imagine it, experience it, believe it!

If you have many addictions, make sure to target one at a time.

When the day to give up your addiction finally arrives; invest as much energy as you can in your new substitute, hobby or desired alternative.

Stay busy, but relax properly.

Keep away from tempting environments until you are ready.

Breathe with positive suggestion in times of need. Get through the moment!

Pay close attention to your out-breath, and divert attention to what is external.

Don't tolerate self-pity. Nip it in the bud with action.

Have faith in your ability to remain in control.

Repeat the suggestion, "I'm in full control," regularly and with belief. What your mind believes, it achieves.

Whenever you think of the old addiction, view the past in black and white, as if watching an old movie.

By dissociating past from present, you become the distant observer rather than the active participant.

> *Towards the end of your hypnotic sessions, give your subconscious some post-hypnotic suggestions specifically geared to what has been given up.*
>
> *Create cues to bring about desired responses in testing situations, for example:*
>
> *"Whenever I smell a cigarette, I feel repulsed and immediately need to drink water; cool, pure, refreshing water."*
>
> *"When my friends smoke cannabis, I feel sorry for them."*
>
> *By staying out of addictions' way, it stays out of yours.*
>
> *Don't put yourself in awkward situations that tempt fate.*
>
> *If you have given up drugs, keep away from the party scene until you are strong enough to resist them.*
>
> *If you're addicted to gambling on horses, steer clear of the bookies.*
>
> *There's no half-way house or compromising with addiction.*
>
> *It's a war that can only be won by annihilating the enemy, completely.*

How to Quit Smoking Permanently

I could use the next three pages of this book explaining the reasons why you should not smoke. But I'm going to spare you the detail because you already know the risks. If smoking doesn't kill you, it will almost certainly knock a few years off your life or possibly lead to serious illness. Most smokers want to quit, but fear is what usually stops them; fear they will gain weight; fear they won't know what to do with their hands; fear their anxiety will spill over; fear they will lose a pleasure in life; or fear they may become depressed. These unrealistic fears are often based on previous experiences of trying to give up. People who are serious about giving up will have attempted it at least twice before. They may have tried patches, gums and inhalers, only to discover that fear was the real factor in making their addiction recommence. The problem with most of these quit smoking products is that they deal only with nicotine withdrawal, and little or no emphasis is placed on the person and their psychological fears. If a person does not have a fear of giving up, it makes the process of quitting that much easier.

Physical addiction can end within a short enough period of time, but psychological addiction takes that little bit longer to overcome. This is why hypnosis is one of the most popular and effective ways to give up smoking. Using imagery instead of willpower, the mind is prepared for the day you are going to quit. This mental preparation allows you to focus on your goal by removing the uncertainty that normally conjures up in the mind when you are about to give up something. The subconscious must come to believe that it has nothing to fear. This is achieved by implanting suggestions and images that promote a smoke-free lifestyle in the weeks and days leading up to the quitting date. Here are some examples of the type of suggestion that can be used:

"I am stronger than ever now. I am ready to stop, forever."

"The habit, the harm and the memory of smoking belong to the past."

"The day to give up is approaching and I am looking forward to it."

"I am focused on giving up, and everyday I grow stronger and stronger."

"I have new, healthy substitutes to replace the dirt, the tar, and the poison."

"The day I quit is the proudest day of my life."

Post-Hypnotic Suggestions and Cues to Help Quit

These can be implanted both in and out of hypnosis:

"It's Friday the seventh. The day I quit. I feel determined and committed."

"Whenever I see a cigarette, it reminds me to breathe deeply and relax."

"The smell of tobacco sickens my stomach."

"When I hold a cigarette, I feel a need to break it in two."
"Smoky environments remind me that I am free."

The Days Before You Quit

Cut down gradually, so that on the day before you quit you are down to one.

Buy some new, fresh clothes to compliment your new lifestyle.

Throw out any photographs of you smoking, unless of course they're sentimental.

Stock up on fruit, vegtables, bottled water and any other healthy substitutions you can think of. If there are certain foods that trigger you to smoke, get rid of them.

Ask your family to support you in whatever way they can. If someone else in your household smokes, tell them that from now on they must smoke outside. Make this a permanent rule!

If you are lucky enough to have all your teeth, make an appointment to get them cleaned.

This will make you feel good. Your teeth will be stain-free and fresh at last. Of course, if you have a fear of dentists, leave it until you have overcome this fear through hypnosis.

Anticipate the healthy smoke-free lifestyle to come with happy expectation. Giving up an addiction is a good thing, so feel good about it.

The Day You Quit

Keep yourself busy and motivated. Fill your day with outdoor activities.

If you have a craving, breathe with suggestion and get through the moment.

Drink plenty of water and fruit juice. Avoid caffeine, alcohol and drinks you would normally associate with smoking.

After each meal, go to the bathroom and brush your teeth (post-hypnotic cue). Enjoy the clean fresh feeling of your mouth and teeth.

Keep away from smoky environments, at least for the first three days. If you encounter one by surprise, hang out with the non-smokers. Participate in activities where it's impossible to smoke, e.g. swimming, tennis etc., or where you use your hands a lot such as writing, gardening, painting, and so on.

The Days After You Quit

When you feel confident enough to be around smokers, have a sympathetic attitude towards them. Feeling sorry for them will strengthen your resolve and give you confidence. Think of yourself as being a source of inspiration to them.

Add up how much you spend on tobacco a month. Lodge this amount to your bank account each month and watch it grow.

If you are a person who enjoys nibbling things, a good idea is to keep healthy substitutes nearby: nuts, raisins, currants, sultanas, prunes, dates, dried mango and banana, carrot and celery sticks. All of these are healthy substitutions which can be kept handy to chew on. Something as simple as a nut can get you through the moment.

Remember, there is always something better to do than smoke. Chewing a piece of gum is better. Having a soft drink is better. Licking an ice-cream is better. If there are no healthy substitutions around and you are stressed out, get through the moment using breath, suggestion and imagination. One puff will sabotage everything, so don't go down that road again.

Acknowledge the fact that your body is healing rapidly now. Within hours nicotine leaves the system and all the major organs of the body begin repairing themselves. You may notice a lot of phlegm and tar being expelled from your lungs. If the weather is cold, make sure you wrap up well and cover your throat. When the lungs expel tar, it can leave them more exposed and susceptible to infection. To some degree, tar provides your lungs with a layer of protection and when this layer has been expelled, it can leave us more prone to catching a cold or chest infection. If you get a chest infection, see a doctor immediately. If you don't, the infection may take much longer than normal to go.

Within a few days, notice the sensitivity of your sense of smell and taste. Put some fresh flowers in the kitchen. Cook yourself tastier dishes. Enjoy being able to savor the taste of food properly, without the foul taste of cigarettes numbing your palate. Entice your taste buds with the food you love and don't be concerned with gaining a few pounds. Quitting smoking doesn't automatically mean you gain weight. The reason people gain weight is because they eat in response to feelings and emotions. The benefits of giving up far outweigh the drawbacks of gaining a couple of pounds.

The Instinctive Yearning

Imagine you were picked up by a helicopter and were flown into the middle of the desert to survive on just a bottle of water for three days. There's a good chance your only concern would be survival, and if this was the case, nicotine withdrawal would be almost certainly non-existent. Preserving water and staying alive would dominate your every thought. Getting out of there would drive your natural instincts. The point I am trying to make is that in order to give up a bad habit such as smoking or excessive drinking, you first need to create in your subconscious a yearning for good health. Once this idea has taken root, nothing can stop it from becoming realized. The *quit smoking script* you are about to use has been designed to instill in your subconscious an instinctive yearning for healthy substitutes. When you have recorded yourself, play it every day for the first week, and then once a week thereafter, until you are satisfied that you feel completely free. Use it to get through any difficult moments that may arise in the first few days. Reinforce your new behavioral program regularly by repeating simple goal-orientated images and suggestions. Think of the money you are going to save, but more importantly, think of the years you are going to gain. Set a date soon and stick to it.

What to Do if You Slip Along the Way

Giving up smoking is by no means an easy task, even for the casual smoker. If temptation or stress get the better of you, don't allow a moment of weakness to start you back smoking again. It's important that you learn from your mistake by taking action immediately. This means going right back to where you left off and using hypnosis daily to strengthen your subconscious program. With smoking, there can be no going back. Even if you fail to give up many times, you must keep pushing yourself until you eventually do. Fear is what stops you giving up, but there is really nothing to fear at all. Thousands of people give up smoking each year and there's no reason why you can't be one of them. Use hypnosis to give up, and you'll be surprised at just how effective it is.

Chapter 13

Ending Alcohol Abuse and Alcoholism

"Drunkenness is nothing but voluntary madness."
Seneca

Understanding Alcohol Abuse and Alcoholism

It is possible to have a drink problem, but not display all the characteristics of *alcoholism*. This is *alcohol abuse*. If you are not dependant on alcohol, but excessive drinking is causing you health, family and social problems, then it is safe to say that you have an alcohol abuse problem. It also makes you a more likely candidate for alcoholism.

People who abuse alcohol experience many of the same symptoms as those who are dependent on it. But what makes them different is that they don't feel the same relentless need to drink, or experience the same withdrawal symptoms as an alcoholic does.

Alcoholism is mainly characterized by a preoccupation with alcohol; or a lack of control over its consumption. If we fail to treat this progressive illness the result is often fatal. Alcoholism is a long term disease that generates a high tolerance and dependency to alcohol. People who abuse alcohol are at much higher risk of suffering from alcoholism than those who don't. If at a young age an individual continually increases their tolerance level through binge drinking, over time their tolerance gets greater, but so too does their dependency. Alcohol dependency takes over the mind and body almost unnoticed, remaining undetected for many years. Both the availability of alcohol and the manner in which it is consumed helps to explain why alcohol abuse and alcoholism are such common problems in society today.

Research indicates that the risk of developing alcoholism runs in certain families. *Genes* can be passed down, but lifestyle is also a major factor. Just because alcoholism runs in some families, it doesn't mean that the child of an alcoholic parent will automatically become an alcoholic. A person may develop alcoholic tendencies even when no one else in their family has a drink problem. But the child or teenager of an alcoholic parent should be made aware that they are more susceptible to its influence than a person whose family's history has no recorded cases of alcoholism.

Drinking in Moderation

Drinking in moderation is relatively harmless and enjoyable. Many people appreciate a nice glass of wine with a good meal, or a cold beer with family and friends on occasion. But of all the drugs that we can potentially become addicted to, alcohol is perhaps the easiest to fall in love with and the hardest to break up with. Almost everywhere we look, bars and restaurants that serve alcohol surround us. Most forms of celebration involve drinking, and advertisers rarely warn us about the dangers excessive drinking causes to health. Because it's widely accepted as something that is just a normal part of everyday living, people often drift into alcoholism blindly, as well as willingly. You start off by going for a few pints at the weekend, enjoying the way it eases your tension and loosens your tongue in conversation. But then something happens in your life, and so you either celebrate or drown your sorrows. The comfort and confidence found in its consumption leads the subconscious to believe that drink is something worthy of attaining, due to its many satisfying uses. This is where the illusion sets in, but others cannot help you. They do not see this transformation happening to your character and by the time they do, it's usually too late. Instead, they offer you another drink, because they know how much you like one. This is how the habit gets fed. Before you know it, you've a real problem on your hands.

Alcoholism and Emotional Disorders

Anxiety and depression among others are common symptoms of alcoholism. A depressed person may begin drinking in order to gain relief from their depression. But alcohol is a natural depressant, which only compounds the problem. Alcohol may provide a temporary release from depression, but this is usually short-lived and eventually leads to dependency. Without first paying attention to the mental health needs of a person with alcoholism, there is little progress made in overcoming the addiction. Even if a person does manage to get to the root cause of their depression through therapeutic means, so long as they continue to drink, depressing their mind with alcohol, there really is no hope of making a full recovery. However, if a person who is not in denial decides that enough is enough, they must target both the cause and symptom simultaneously. The emotional problem may be causing the drinking and vice versa, so both must be dealt with together. But unfortunately they are usually not. This is why so many recovering alcoholics suffer relapses. When a person is in recovery, they are more prone to relapses. Relapses often convince the recovering alcoholic that they have no option left but to stop drinking. The process of recovery should involve group support, rehabilitation programs, Alcoholics Anonymous and so forth.

If you are dependant on alcohol and need help, please consult your doctor immediately and find out what treatments are available to you. Then contact a therapist specializing in alcohol addiction and remain in treatment until you feel that you are physically and emotionally better again.

The Signs and Symptoms of Alcohol Abuse and Alcoholism

Drinking to feel normal.

Drinking to make problems go away.

Drinking alone.

Drinking in the morning.

Drinking for the sake of it rather than the enjoyment of it.

Drinking all night and not feeling drunk, or drinking yourself sober.

Craving alcohol in the same way you crave for food or water.

When you start drinking, you find it hard to stop.

Lying to your family about your habit.

Hiding drink away from family.

Having blackouts, not knowing how you got home, forgetting commitments.

Arriving late to work because of drink.

Spending less time with your family.

Being abusive or aggressive while under the influence.

Losing interest in life, but not in alcohol.

Suffering withdrawals such as shaking, sweating, panic, anxiety, or depression.

Denying you have symptoms of alcoholism. Most alcoholics don't want or believe they need help.

Noticing that your tolerance is on the increase.

Giving up hobbies and activities to drink or recover from drink.

Becoming annoyed when someone or something interferes with, or if people comment on your drinking habits.

Feeling a compulsion to drink.

Feeling guilty about drinking.

The Effects of Alcohol Abuse and Alcoholism

Here are just some of the effects of heavy, consistent drinking:

Risk of heart attack and stroke. High blood pressure.

Alcoholic hepatitis. Inflammation and cirrhosis of the liver.

Jaundice (yellowing of the skin).

Memory loss and dementia.

Gastritis (inflammation of the stomach lining).

Pancreatic disease.

Poor absorption of vitamins, minerals and nutrients.

Increased risk of cancer.

Damage to the nervous system.

Diabetes complications.

Seizures (delirium tremens).

Paralysis of the eye muscles.

Sexual dysfunction; impotence for men and menstruation problems for women.

Poor bone production; thinning of bones and increased risk of fracture.

Birth defects; Fetal alcohol syndrome.

Higher risk of suicide.

Risk of developing emotional disorders or exacerbating existing ones.

An increased likelihood of new addictions developing.

How to End Alcohol Abuse

Self-hypnosis in alliance with professional help is effective in the treatment of alcohol abuse, but should only be used as a complement in the treatment of alcoholism.

Overcoming alcoholism is a serious venture for anyone to undertake and is done with the help of healthcare professionals and family support. This is what you must do in order to overcome alcohol abuse:

Instill a desire to end your addiction during self-hypnosis. Want it badly and be prepared to make sacrifices. A strong desire to either cut down or give up completely must be present in your subconscious.

End the abuse by making a decision to stop it, period.

Evaluate the alternatives and substitutes available to you. Find the ones that have the capacity to fulfill your needs.

Set a date to cut down or give up, and focus on that date intently both in and out of trance.

Pre-empt how your future is going to look by imagining big, bright, colorful images of you drinking in moderation and enjoying your new substitutes.

When the day comes to give up, invest as much energy as you can in your new substitute, hobby, or desired alternative.

Breathe with positive suggestion in times of need and get through the moment. Pay close attention to your out-breath and divert focus to the external world. Do not tolerate self-pity for a second. Nip it in the bud with action.

Have faith in your ability to remain in control. Regularly repeat the suggestion, "I'm in full control."

Whenever you think of your old habits, view the past in black and white. Drain the life out of the old images that once drove your dependency by turning them into black and white. Then reduce them in size until they are insignificant. This is a good way to desensitize old unwanted images or memories you may unconsciously associate with alcohol.

By staying out of alcohol's way, it will stay out of yours. Don't put yourself in awkward situations that only tempt fate.

Examples of Post-Hypnotic Suggestions and Cues to Help End Alcohol Abuse

Here are some post-hypnotic suggestions to implant during self-hypnosis:

"Whenever I drink I feel satisfied after having just two."
"Every time a glass touches my lips, I drink very slowly."
"The smell of alcohol makes me crave water."

You Don't Have to Fight Alone

Find new things to do and new places to go. Keep away from the bars, especially during the first two to three weeks of recovery. Think of family and friends and don't be too proud to ask them for support. Alcoholism is a disease, and treatment must be aimed at teaching you how to manage it. *Alcoholics Anonymous* helps many people to stop drinking and remain sober. They offer support around the clock; so if you still struggle or need someone to talk to, help is just a phone call away. They also offer support to family members who find it difficult to cope with the stress of living with an alcoholic.

The first most important step in treating alcoholism is recognizing that the problem exists. Then with a strong desire to change you must confront it head on, with an unconscious longing for good health. You must do whatever it takes to rid your body of the poison that once provided pleasure and find new ways of satisfying your inner thirst without alcohol. Be on your guard at all times, especially when you are doing well and staying off the drink. In moments of happiness or weakness it is easy to accept a drink from a friend or stranger without even realizing it. You look down and there it is in your hand, then the guilt sets in and you think to yourself, "I'd better drink it," or "I don't want to offend them by not drinking it."

The next thing you know it, it has passed your lips and the cycle has begun again. This is how easily recovery gets sabotaged and is why it's necessary to remain in treatment for a long time, if not for life. It all depends on the person and their capabilities, as well as their family and social background. Some people recover quickly, but for others it takes much longer. One thing for sure is that recovery must remain consistent, with on-going help from family, friends and support groups.

What to Do if You Have a Relapse

Having a relapse should not be viewed as failure. It happens because of human weakness, and because alcohol addiction is one of the hardest habits to break. If you suffer a relapse, seek professional help immediately; do everything in your power to get back on the wagon. Being hard on yourself achieves nothing, neither does self-pity. If you let yourself down by drinking alcohol when you shouldn't, learn from your mistake and move on. How you deal with your problem is the measure of your worth. It's you against alcohol, and you must win.

Alcohol Cessation Script

(Use one of the deepeners from Chapter 5 at the beginning of this script)

You have come to the point in your life, where you are now ready to stop drinking, finally, and forever. You know why you must stop, and you are also deeply aware of the effect it is having on your overall health. Now you long for a healthy mind, and a healthy body, a healthy mind, and a healthy body (Pause). And you are finding strength with each day that passes, to overcome fear, and remain free of drink. And what you are discovering, is that you have the power and the ability to overcome. Why? Because now you are determined, and committed, committed, and determined, relaxing deeper, and deeper now, just letting go, all the way, down, down, deeper and deeper. For you are so relaxed, so very, very relaxed, while you just flow and drift, drift and flow (Pause). And as you continue relaxing, become aware, of just how powerful your subconscious mind is, and trust in its ability to get you through this time. Your subconscious is now making important changes on your behalf, changes which you approve of, changes which you desire, relaxing more and more, deeper and deeper. You know that inside you, there are resources which you can draw upon, and energy, which you can draw upon. Feel this energy moving inside your head now, and allow its force to reverberate through your mind. All your mental energy is now being focused on health and happiness. You crave health, you crave life, and you crave water, cool, pure, refreshing water. And imagine for me now, a glass of cool, pure, refreshing water. Imagine picking up the glass. Feel the coldness of it in your hand (Pause) and now as it touches your dry lips (Pause). Imagine drinking it down. Enjoy the cool sensation as it runs down your throat, and as the longing inside you gets satisfied. And whenever you see alcohol, you find that you immediately crave water, cool, pure, refreshing water. And whenever you are offered alcohol, you find it very easy to say, "No thank you." And you take a great deal of pleasure in saying, "No thank you." Why? Because now you are free, and are able to enjoy a social occasion free from the former slave master of alcohol (Pause). So as you continue to become more secure within yourself, more confident, more self-assured, realize that you are in full control all the time. No matter what happens, you are always in full control. You choose the way you want to live, and you control what goes in and out of the precious body you have. And the more you breathe, the more you relax, and the more you relax, the better you feel. And the more you breathe, the more you relax, and the more you relax, the better you feel. In your mind's eye, you now see yourself poised and confident, calm and relaxed, and always in full control. These pictures of you are big, bright and colorful (Pause). Your subconscious mind is now absorbing these images of you, and is shaping your behavioral program to suit your needs. And the more you learn about yourself, the more confident you become. And you understand deeply, that you are now alcohol free. Completely, and totally free. The habit, the harm and the memory of alcohol now belong to the past. This is your moment, you know what you want. You are now and forever a happy, natural and permanent non-drinker. Rest for a while now...

Chapter 14

Ending Drug Addiction

"The mind is capable of achieving greater highs without drugs."
Cathal O'Briain

Understanding Drug Addiction

Drug addiction is a condition characterized by an overuse of drugs, despite a person knowing the unhealthy consequences of taking them. You can be dependent on drugs without actually being addicted. For example, someone taking prescribed drugs over lengthy periods of time for a specific illness would fit into this category. The addictive nature of drugs varies from substance to substance and from person to person, but there are also certain drugs with addictive qualities which are roughly the same for everyone. For example, cocaine for most is addictive, but for others, gradual exposure to pharmaceutical drugs is just as addictive.

Physical dependency occurs when the body develops a high tolerance to drugs through prolonged usage. The drug no longer satisfies mental and physical needs without ultimately triggering symptoms of withdrawal and biological dependency. *Psychological dependency* occurs when the subconscious believes that it needs a drug in order to fulfill its desires. Addicts nurture their needs through ritualistic misuse of narcotics, which is likely to make a person become addicted faster than actual physical addiction will. This does not apply certain drugs like *cocaine* or *heroin*, but to other narcotics, such as *cannabis, ecstasy,* or *LSD*. Psychologists classify certain drugs like *LSD* or *magic mushrooms* as being *non-addictive*. Some experts on addiction believe that the above mentioned drugs do not create mental or physical dependency at all. Nonetheless, these *mind-bending* drugs still cause major disturbances in the mind by producing suitable conditions for mental illness to occur. Even drugs labeled milder, such as cannabis, have been found to cause severe thought and mood disorders. The danger with calling drugs milder is that it can mislead people into thinking they are relatively safe to use on a daily basis. Experts have proven that cannabis is addictive and there is much clinical evidence linking it to mental illness, particularly *psychosis, schizophrenia, anxiety,* and *depression.* Whether drugs are mild or soft is irrelevant. Even prescription drugs will cause mental and physical illness if abused for long enough. By admitting you have a problem, you take the first step to recovery. By ignoring it, you deprive yourself of the chance to live properly.

Substance Abuse and Emotional Disorders

Substance abuse can occur with or without dependency and with or without addiction. It is any use of a substance, which causes more harm than good. It is also a maladaptive way to behave as it negatively affects the user and those around them. Continued substance abuse will generally lead to dependency and addiction. Most people at some point in their lives encounter drugs: at a party, in a friend's house, or a nightclub. It's easy to see how the sensations of being high, along with social pressure, can influence a person into taking drugs. Life's temptations can be irresistible at times. The fact that people are human is enough to make everyone vulnerable to the effects of substance abuse.

Low serotonin levels can cause depression. So if your neurotransmitters are getting regularly drained, over time psychological problems can develop as a result of cell and nerve damage. One thing to be said for alcohol is that you at least know what you are drinking most of the time. With drugs, however, you take a major risk whenever you get high on them. This is because you don't know where they come from, what's gone into them, or what they are doing to your mind and body.

Getting High isn't all it's Cracked Up To Be

When clients come to me with drug addiction, I get them to explore the sensation of being high by recalling it to their mind in hypnosis. Here are some of the types of responses I'm usually given:

> *"I feel as though I haven't a problem or worry in the world."*
> *"I feel confident and want to dance."*
> *"I feel detached from myself."*
> *"I just want to go off into my own world."*

When they have given me their various impressions of being high, I then ask them to describe the way they feel in the days after taking drugs. Here are some typical answers:

> *"I feel fine for the first two days and then I get really low."*
> *"I lose my appetite and go into myself."*
> *"I get very depressed and sometimes I fly off the handle."*
> *'I worry about money because I've spent it all on drugs.'*

Then I respond by asking, "Do you think the high that you described to me moments ago is worth the low that you feel in the days that follow?"

And of course the answer is always "No."

When treating cannabis addicts for psychological problems I get them to describe what being stoned is like for them. Here are some of the answers I am given:

> *"I feel relaxed and chilled out."*
> *"I don't really now how I feel. I'm just stoned."*
> *"My head gets dopey and I feel hungry."*

I tell them that what they just described to me as *being stoned* is really not that amazing at all. They tend to agree.

Every artificial sensation that you feel when you are high can be felt naturally at even higher levels in self-hypnosis. Half of the high in taking drugs is just placebo effect and the other half is the drug itself. Even the anticipation of taking a drug is enough to bring on its effect. The reality is that they make you low rather than high. Even when a person is high, they still go through phases of *paranoia, detachment* and *introversion*. It literally sucks the life out of people by draining the energy reserves of the mind, and for what? So you can escape from reality? If you continually escape from reality, it only makes it that bit harder to come back to it. The mind that aspires to be free of drugs has the potential to be realized fully. The high that you feel in self-hypnosis is far greater that anything a drug can ever provide. You can achieve heightened awareness and elevated happiness while in the hypnotic state. Naturally-induced trance must become your new substitute for drugs.

You control the shape of your reality. Substance abuse takes away this control by shaping reality to suit its needs. This is how people get stuck in a rut, and is where the process of maturation gets put on hold, sometimes for life. In the same way that food cannot satisfy feelings, neither can drugs. Once you finish consuming the drugs and the effect wears off, the feelings and emotions come back, and are usually stronger. This is where the danger lies.

The Signs and Symptoms of Drug Addiction and Substance Abuse

Inability to relax or find pleasure without drugs.

Mood swings, irritable behavior, paranoia, immaturity or bad attitude.

Talking about drugs all the time or pressuring others to use them.

Making inappropriate remarks or saying the wrong thing at the wrong time.

Not looking after physical appearance, e.g. teeth, breath, body odor and so on.

Neglecting family and friends to be with people taking drugs.

Behaving secretively and suspiciously. Keeping money aside for the habit.

Using drugs first thing in the morning and last thing at night.

General lack of interest in things. No motivation, tired and grumpy.

Sleeping all day and becoming a night owl.

More susceptible to having angry outbursts, crying, shouting, etc.

Less likely to participate in intellectual activities.

Lack of co-ordination and balance.

After an argument turning to drugs to alleviate stress.

Using drugs as a substitute for happiness.

Not wanting to quit because the desire simply isn't there.

Anxiety, stress, panic, fear, poor energy, insomnia and many more.

The Effects of Drug Addiction

When the brain receives a stimulus it likes, it tends to want it more. Addictive drugs enter the body through a variety of routes. Then they make their way to the brain through the bloodstream. Drugs attempt to mimic the brain's natural chemicals and systematic processes, instilling in the mind a desire to take even more drugs. But the addict feels the effects of drug addition on more than just one level. Personal health, family, friends and social life all can be affected. Here are just a few examples of its effects:

Loss of love, mental and physical health, house, job, partner, sex-life, friendships due to drugs or financial problems relating to drugs.

Inability to mature and become the individual you are capable of being.

Risk of heart attack and stroke, high blood pressure.

Memory loss and dementia.

Damage to the nervous system.

Pregnancy complications and birth defects.

Risk of developing emotional disorders or exacerbating existing ones.

An increased likelihood of new addictions developing.

Developing a character or personality disorder.

Increased likelihood of hurting yourself or those around you through accidental injury.

Users of cannabis, grass and hallucinogenic drugs can experience flashbacks and unprovoked reminders of a bad trip experienced months previously.

Heroin withdrawal can cause trembling, shaking, sweating, muscle cramps, vomiting, diarrhea and convulsions. With heroin addiction there is also the risk of catching infectious diseases or HIV.

The Effects of Cocaine Abuse

Due to the sudden upsurge in cocaine availability and abuse in recent years, my hypnotherapy practice now receives more cocaine addicts than ever before. Ordinary people can get caught up in this pointless, life-numbing addiction. Fatigue, stress and a stifled mental economy takes its toll upon the user. This is clearly marked by a pale, withdrawn look upon the face. There is also a lack of energy and life in their character, especially when away from the drug. But this makes them all the more driven to participate in taking cocaine. It is usually at the point of financial ruin that people begin seeking professional help, but by then, the abuse has usually gone way too far, where it now impedes on every aspect of living. Ongoing therapy must begin here to stop the addiction.

Cocaine is a powerful drug that stimulates the brain and activates the central nervous system. Due to cocaine's anesthetic qualities, it is used in surgery for minor operations on areas such as the eye and nose, but has very little medical use otherwise. Besides being a highly addictive narcotic, cocaine is also quite expensive in comparison to other recreational drugs of its class. For this reason addicts often find themselves in financial trouble, only adding to their fatigue, restlessness and irritability. What starts out as a bit of fun can sometimes end up a serious addiction. In the past I've heard clients say "My habit's under control," when I know they can barely afford to pay me for therapy. This is the illusion created in the minds of those who refuse to recognize that they have a problem. A wake-up call in life such as a birth or sudden death in a family can sometimes be enough to inspire a person's subconscious to change, or move away from addiction. For some, a shock to their system may be the only way of actually giving up. Of course the shock-factor element may also create the opposite effect; worsening the addiction because the person suffering tries to escape their problems by increasing their cocaine intake.

One reason why cocaine is so popular is because of the effect that it creates in the mind. With other recreational drugs such as ecstasy tablets, the effect in the mind is different in so far as it's encouraged by certain types of music and atmosphere. This means the user will mostly restrict their habit to the weekend, when the nightclubs are open and parties are happening. But with cocaine, the user can take it anywhere, or at any time of the day. One person might have some at a friend's party, whereas another will snort a line just before an important business meeting in an effort to appear more confident. To the observer, someone taking cocaine might just appear to be more alert and confident. This is why users desire its effect. It allows the user access to artificial confidence without appearing to others that they are taking drugs.

Cocaine use forms a strong addiction within a short period of time. Taking the drug repeatedly at increasingly higher amounts can eventually lead to a state of despair, paranoia or even psychosis. It's a far reaching problem affecting many countries, both rich and poor, and its widespread abuse is growing rapidly, with a much greater variety of users now than ever before. Not surprising, when you consider the availability of this highly addictive and dangerous drug to all classes in society.

Those who snort cocaine say it makes them feel bright, alert, interested and confident. What they actually refer to in scientific terms is just a build up of dopamine, causing continuous stimulation of receiving neurons, resulting in alertness and euphoria. For the sake of feeling confident, alert and euphoric, cocaine leaves the user open to many disturbing risks, and at dangerously high levels. Here are just a few of the problems it causes:

Heart attacks, seizures, strokes, increased heart rate, constricted blood vessels, high or low blood pressure, and respiratory failure. Chest pain associated with cocaine use is now a very common problem in accident and emergency departments.

Dysfunctional nervous system, digestive problems, headache, and nausea. Because the user often has no appetite, this can lead to malnourishment and general physical neglect. Eating disorders such as anorexia and bulimia have been linked to cocaine abuse.

Over stimulation of the sympathetic (arousal) system causes abnormal heart rhythms. Those rhythms can cause sudden death.

Mixing alcohol and cocaine damages the liver and also increases the risk of sudden death.

Snorting cocaine can lead to loss of smell and taste, nosebleeds, infected throat, problems swallowing, and regular chest infections.

Cocaine use during pregnancy can increase complications for mother and baby. It can affect the developing baby directly, mentally and physically, as well as increasing the risk of miscarriage.

Anxiety, depression, panic attacks, fears, phobias, paranoia, drug psychosis, mania, erratic behavior, loss of interest in life and so on.

How to End Cocaine and Drug Abuse

Instill a desire to end your addiction while in Self-Hypnosis. Want it badly and be prepared to make sacrifices. A strong desire to either cut down or give up completely must be present in your subconscious and kept present.

End the abuse by making a decision to stop it, period!

Evaluate the alternatives and substitutes available to you. Find the ones that have the capacity to fulfill your needs.

Set a date for when you are going to give up and focus on that date intently, both in and out of trance.

Pre-empt how your future will look by imagining big, bright, colorful images of you enjoying your new, healthy substitutes.

When the day comes to give up, invest as much energy as you can in your new substitute, hobby, or desired alternative.

Breathe with positive suggestion in times of need and get through the moment. Pay close attention to your out-breath and divert attention to the external world.

Have faith in your ability to remain in control. Repeat the suggestion, "I'm in full control," regularly and with belief in what you are saying.

Whenever you think of your old habits, view the past in black and white. Drain the life out of the old images that once drove your dependency by reducing them in size until they are insignificant. Then throw them into a bin, or burn them.

Don't put yourself in awkward situations that tempt fate. Keep away from the drug scene, even if it means losing a few friends. If they are genuine friends, they will help you by not tempting you.

If you are addicted to the likes of crack cocaine or heroin, get yourself into detoxification or onto a methadone program. The aim of detoxification is to relieve withdrawal symptoms while you adjust to a drug-free lifestyle. It is not in itself a treatment for addiction, but is the first step taken towards long-term treatment that is either drug-free or with the use of medication.

Detoxification programs usually last between three to six months. Methadone treatment is safe, effective and does not interfere with everyday activities. The medication is taken orally and relieves withdrawal symptoms for up to thirty-six hours. Craving is what causes people to relapse and this is why methadone is so effective; it stops the craving. Combined with therapy and self-therapy, methadone treatment is a good way to overcome heroin addiction.

Use self-hypnosis in conjunction with your recovery and stay strong. You have the ability.

Examples of Post Hypnotic Suggestions to Help End Drug Abuse

"When I hear people talking about drugs, I am instantly reminded of poverty."

"The smell of cannabis makes me crave fresh air."

"When I see cocaine, I think of my children and my duty as a father/mother to them."

You Have a Choice

Remember, getting high isn't all it cracked up to be, and if you are addicted, know that you have the ability to give up the habit, permanently. But first you must build up the courage to say, *"I'm ready to make a sacrifice in order to change my life for the better."*

It would be nice to think that in a year you could be looking back on this time, saying to yourself, *"I did it."*

Now that would be real change.

If you are a drug addict, the path to freedom is not as far away as it may look. But first you must realize that as a free person you have a choice. You have the right to choose what is good and what is bad for you. By choosing to remain addicted, you deprive yourself of the chance of ever reaching your true potential. But it's not just about you. It's also about the ones you love and cherish in your life.

This chapter provides the following script to help you release your addiction, but please be ready to seek professional help if necessary to help you go the full distance.

Drugs Cessation Script

(Use one of the deepeners from Chapter 5 at the beginning of this script)

Because good health is a state of mind, you can now begin to think healthily. The life that you have left behind, has been left behind for a reason – it was ruining you. The ones you love could also see that it was ruining you. But that life was discarded and thrown away, because it was useless and expensive, heart-breaking, and troubling. It was worn out and beaten, shameful and depressing. But now it's over, because you have decided that enough is enough. And this time you have really stopped, and there is no more turning back for you. You were born to be free, and to remain free. This is your birthright and is why you have made the final decision, to release your mind from drug addiction, finally, and forever, finally, and forever. Relaxing deeper, and deeper still, just letting go, completely (Pause). And as you bask now in relaxation, realize that your friends and acquaintances want you to overcome the addiction as well. They value you, and love you, and want to see you getting well. They will see the real you emerging, more and more with each day that passes. For you are the happy one, the confident one, the relaxed one. You know that you can be anything you want to be, and what you most desire to be now, is drug-free, and healthy. Now you enjoy having a good time with friends without feeling the former need for drugs. The conversation is better, more intellec-tually stimulating. Eye contact is always maintained, and so is composure, because now you are sharp, focused, relaxed, and free. Sharp, focused, relaxed, and free. And the more you breathe, the more you relax, and the more you relax, the better you feel. Now it will be easier than ever, for you to handle your responsi-bilities more effectively than before, because now, you have full control over everything you do, where you go, who you meet, and what you say (Pause). You know deep in your heart that the only way to be truly free of drugs, is by simply avoiding them: period. This realization is in your subconscious, and you are finding it easy to stay out of harm's way. Each time you encounter drugs, you have a choice, and you always choose to remain free. When you are free, you are at your natural best, and now you wholeheartedly embrace responsibility. You are entering a world of new, exciting experience; a world of opportunity and inner awareness, where eating, sleeping and working all conform to healthy living. The way you walk, talk, dress and act, reflect your sober state of wellbeing. Everyday you are looking better, and better, healthier, and healthier, stronger, and stronger (Pause). Your powerful mind is healing the damage that was done, and is supplying your brain with new, fresh cells, and happy, positive thoughts. And each and every time you enter into this relaxed state, you find that you go deeper and deeper, deeper and deeper. And every time you enter this relaxed state, you find that you get stronger, and stronger, stronger and stronger (Pause). Look to the future with confidence, and enjoy your new, healthy lifestyle in the present. You are free to go ahead and enjoy life to the full. All the restrictions have been lifted. There are no obstacles in your way. You are now and forever, happy, natural, and free. Your subconscious mind is now making these powerful suggestions a permanent part of your internal program. Just rest ever deeper now...

Chapter 15

Managing Weight the Easy and Natural Way

"Imagine yourself thin."
Cathal O'Briain

Pleasure-Seeking Animals

By nature, you are a pleasure-seeking animal. Mental energy is driven by an unconscious need to satisfy age-old instinctive longings for nourishment, replenishment, stimulation and relaxation. As food is central to survival, it isn't long before the link between food and pleasure establishes itself within the developing mind. And so, the pleasure-seeking cycle of life begins: firstly in the *nutritional zone,* with continuous use of the mouth, lips, tongue and swallowing action to transmit powerful messages of satisfaction to the maturing mind. Then secondly it begins in the *sexual zone,* where even the task of bowel control can provide a sense of pleasure within the developing mind. In an unrelenting campaign of search and devour, instinctive mental energy flows back and forth like the tide as it untiringly seeks out new objects for gratification. Providing there is no overindulgence in any one particular method of attaining this goal, this natural, healthy, and productive drive can remain satisfied throughout life. What interferes with the pleasure-seeking ambitions of your mind is the human tendency to overindulge or attach guilt to pleasure. Both tendencies directly oppose your mind's normal, healthy intentions. This can lead pleasure to becoming self-punishment or unnecessary reward. When satisfaction can no longer be attained through healthy means, due to a fixated or stagnated drive, the sufferer often does not recogise it as punishment. Nor is it understood as self-sabotage; for if it was, pleasure would remain pleasure. Negative habitual thinking must come to an end before one can correctly understand and feel true pleasure.

Denying yourself pleasure is useful for disciplining the mind; and those who practice self-control are to be commended, for that is pleasurable to them. But to deny yourself the natural and basic things you unconsciously wish for (whether that be food, walking, singing, or having sex) is a strict regime of self-control that can sometimes result in the mind seeking pleasure through its own feelings and impulses. Large amounts of energy can become consumed in the maintainance of a symptom that satisfies the mind at a deeper level.

Every individual has a code of ethics that is personal to them; and every time you follow internal hungers, you make moralistic choices. But the right balance must be struck, for too much or too little pleasure can be equally bad for your health. Follow your drive, as it introduces you to all the wonderful pleasures of life; but know when to say enough is enough. Do not combine guilt with pleasure, for together they work against your natural hungers. Your life is for savouring and exploring, and you are programmed to explore; for like the rest of us, you are a pleasure-seeking animal.

Healthy Body, Healthy Mind

Most people have a natural desire to look and feel good. Whether you want to lose a few stone or simply shed a couple of pounds, this chapter along with its accompanying weight reduction script will help you reach your goals, providing of course you stick to the rules. You won't be left feeling deprived, because this is not a diet. It is simply an effective psychological way to discard excess weight permanently while still being able to enjoy the food you desire to eat.

About Diets

To put it simply, diets do not work. Even if you do manage to reduce weight, there's a good chance you'll put it back on and even quicker than you lost it. I'm sure you've tried a number of diets in the past only to discover that you were feeling miserable about yourself at the end of each one. If your goal is to manage your weight and feel happy, all you have to do is change the way you feel about yourself and how you react in the presence of food. Dieting makes losing weight appear a momentous task, but the reality is that weight management isn't really that hard. By putting into practice the simple guide you're about to learn, you will find that the answer to reaching your desired weight lies not in cruel diets, but comes about through changing how you think and respond to food. By changing how you react in the presence of food, you instantly change your relationship with it. It then becomes your friend instead of your foe. A healthy relationship with food must ensue before taking any steps towards weight reduction. It's not you against food, but is rather you learning to love and respect food and the wonderful body you are blessed with.

Because diets don't work, I'm now going to outline eight easy steps to permanent weight reduction that really work. First of all I want you to learn the steps off by heart, because they are all you are ever going to need to discard excess weight and keep it off!

Eight Easy Steps to Weight Reduction

Step 1:   *Imagine you are getting thinner and thinner.*

Step 2:   *Never eat in response to feelings or emotions.*

Step 3:   *Breathe with positive suggestion to relieve cravings.*

Step 4:   *Eat the food you love and desire to taste.*

Step 5:   *Eat when you are hungry.*

Step 6:   *Chew slowly and taste your food.*

Step 7:   *Stop eating the second you are no longer hungry.*

Step 8:   *Exercise with ease.*

Step 1: Imagine You are Getting Thinner and Thinner

Remember that imagination is the language of the subconscious. By knowing that your imagination has the capacity to turn you into what you desire, you are already halfway there. Every time you present an image of a fat person to your mind, you unintentionally program that image into your subconscious. Because the subconscious has no ability to reason, it accepts this image as being true and then goes about creating a behavioral program to suit that very image. Your mind will always believe what you present to it in the form of suggestion and image. So, if you continually tell it that you are fat while constantly imagining you are, you leave it no choice but to create a program to fit that image. The mental program you create is what keeps you at the weight you are. Your mind simply does what you ask it to; which is to maintain and work towards an image of an overweight person. What you perceive in your imagination tends to become reality. And the more you dwell upon negative self-images, the greater their chance becomes of being realized. So if you imagine you are thin as much as possible, the mind naturally creates a healthy program to suit those images. Find a picture of when you were at your slimmest (if you have one) and stick it on the wall in your room where you can focus on it before inducing hypnosis. This will help you to render up images in the hypnotic state of how you choose to look soon. Dwell, dwell and dwell upon the thought, idea and image of thinness.

When you look in the mirror, tell yourself that you have a wonderful body. It's very important that you love and respect the body you have by removing the critical observer in your mind. People can be very hard on themselves, using all kinds of nasty words when describing their shape. You must remove these words permanently from your dictionary of self-abuse. These harsh words affect your behavioral program and also how you respond to food. You wouldn't call someone else a fat slob to their face, so the same should go for you and the manner in which you communicate internally. By making your body your best friend it will work much more effectively in helping you reach your desired goal of being slim and healthy. Love the mind and body you have at all times.

Step 2: Never Eat in Response to Feelings or Emotions

Emotional eating is one of the main reasons why people can't lose weight and keep it off. Feelings and emotions are there for a reason and no amount of food is ever going to satisfy a feeling or an emotion. When you eat in response to emotions, it's very hard to hear your body say "I'm no longer hungry."

You just keep on shovelling it in until you feel bloated and wheezy, and usually wind up feeling worse than you did before you started eating. Feelings and emotions are a call to action. They are a signal for you to do something about your present situation. When you eat in response to emotions, you only end up creating more ill-feelings by not dealing with the original ones appropriately. Added to this then is also the painful knowledge that once again you've allowed yourself to eat too much because of a feeling or emotion.

If you feel lonely, it's a signal. It's a signal to do something in order to change the feeling in your body. Picking up the telephone or talking to a friend would be a good way of responding to such a feeling, but opening the fridge door would not.

You must not allow feelings and emotions to make you eat. This is when you must be at your strongest and do whatever is necessary to handle the feeling. The next time you feel bored or lonely I want you to say to yourself, *"This is important! My feelings are trying to tell me something. I need to take action."*

Step 3: Breathe with Positive Suggestion to Relieve Cravings

If at any stage you feel a craving or an urge to gorge on food, I want you to do this:

Inhale slowly and say in your mind the word, *"Calm."* Then exhale slowly and smoothly and say in your mind, *"and relaxed."*

Repeat this a few times until the craving disappears.

This will get you over the desire to binge, because your breathing will direct your attention away from food. If you have time on your hands, get yourself into hypnosis and implant suggestions for satisfaction and relaxation. This will get you through the craving easily and comfortably.

Step 4: Eat the Food You Love and Desire to Taste

If I was to say to you, *"I don't want you to eat chocolate and sweets,'* the very images of what I have asked you not to eat would naturally pop into your head. As you know, the imagination is very powerful; if there is a battle between will and imagination, imagination always wins the day. For this reason it's important to eat what you want to eat and not what you think you should be eating. When diets tell us not to eat this or that because they are forbidden foods, it only makes us obsess and think about them all the more. It's this very obsession that leads people to binge eating. Once an idea or image takes root in your subconscious, it must be carried out in reality.

When you practice eating what you want, within a short space of time a balanced and nutritional diet is encouraged to develop. Healthy eating choices become more attractive when you allow your body to make natural decisions about eating. If you were to eat chocolate all day, your body would eventually long for something nutritious. This is why a balanced diet develops once you stop forbidding certain foods.

Eat the food you enjoy. That way you rid your mind of the obsessive longing that is at the center of dieting. By nature, humans are pleasure-seeking animals. If you remove pleasure from your life, it results in anxiety. Food is a pleasure and will remain a pleasure so long as you continue to enjoy it. If you follow these eight steps with imagination, you will always be able to enjoy the food you love.

Step 5: Eat When You Are Hungry

There is a big difference between eating when you are hungry and eating for the sake of it. The reason people eat for the sake of it is because they are choosing to ignore their body's natural hunger signals. Learning to listen to your body comes with being friends with it. If you love and listen to your body, then you will know the difference between real hunger and wanting to eat for the sake of it. But when you are genuinely hungry, it is important to eat.

Another reason diets don't work is because when you starve yourself throughout the day, or only eat at designated times, your body then stores fat for fear it might not see food again. If you eat when you are genuinely hungry, your body does not store fat and can remove excess fat easily. A fast metabolism can burn calories easily, but if you don't eat when you are hungry your metabolism slows down in order to conserve energy. By not eating when you are hungry you ignore the natural processes of your mind and body and this can lead to feeling hungry when you are actually not. By obeying the laws of real hunger and not going against this natural process, you speed up your metabolism and also remove negative behavioral patterns about food.

Step 6: Chew Slowly and Taste Your Food

One of the big reasons people put on weight is because they eat too quickly and gobble the food as if the meal were going to be taken away from them. For people who claim to love food, we don't even allow ourselves to taste it half the time. From now on when you are eating what you desire to eat, I want you to consciously slow down your chewing to a snail's pace. Then I want you to taste each and every mouthful individually. Think about all the different ingredients that go to make up the wonderful taste of the food you are eating. Allow it to be broken down properly with your teeth. Science has proven that we can aid digestion by chewing our food properly. When you chew quite deliberately and enjoy each and every mouthful, you are in a much better position to recognize the signal from your stomach that says, *"I am no longer hungry."* Make sure to chew very slowly and very consciously!

Step 7: Stop Eating the Second You Are No Longer Hungry

Up to now you may not have been able to recognize the signal being sent from your stomach to your brain that says, *"I am no longer hungry."*

In the past, it is likely that you ignored this signal even when it came to your brain. In the future, when the signal comes that you are no longer hungry, *stop eating!* If there is food left on the plate, wrap it up and put it away until you are genuinely hungry again. You must work with your body and the signals it regularly sends, and if it says to you *"I am no longer hungry,"* then this is a clear signal to stop eating. Over time your body will grow accustomed to recognizing these clear signals and you will enjoy the feeling of being in full control. The most important thing to remember is: the second you feel as though you are no longer hungry, stop eating!

Step 8: Exercise With Ease

Exercise is important but doesn't mean overdoing it at the gym or running five miles a day. It simply means moving your body in more ways than you are doing now. I recommend going for a brisk walk every day to begin with. Consistency is key and it is better to exercise for fifteen minutes every day than to damage your joints jogging twice a week when you are not physically up to it. All I want you to do is increase your heart rate easily and gently and over time as you get fitter. Whether you exercise regularly or not, make sure you drink plenty of water; it helps flush toxins and cellulite from your body and keeps you hydrated.

You will achieve success but you must give it time. Take it in your stride and enjoy this new way of thinking and responding to food. Diets will become a thing of the past once you find yourself persevering with ease and enjoyment and remember to stop eating as soon as satisfaction replaces your hunger. If you stick to the rules, this is the easiest form of weight-reduction in the world. All that I ask of you is to make the eight steps a permanent part of your mental programming through self-hypnosis. The world is your oyster; but please remember when to stop eating it.

Love the body you have, no matter what your shape or size is. Treat it with the same respect that you now give your mind in self-hypnosis and tell yourself each day that you have an attractive body. Listen to your stomach as well as your core feelings and know the difference between boredom and hunger. Feelings are a call to action. Action speaks louder than food. Remember, there is no amount of food that can ever satisfy a feeling or emotion, so don't go down the road of self-disgust by stuffing your guts to feel happy. It doesn't work, and you know it. No food should ever be forbidden, nor should it make you feel guilty. Food is for nutrition and pleasure and will always be enjoyed so long as you make it your friend and not your enemy. Getting slim and healthy is easy and enjoyable with self-hypnosis. By passing down images of a thin you to your deeper mind on a daily basis, you give the subconscious no option but to do everything in its power to make real these images of a slimmer, healthier and happier you.

The following script may provide varying degrees of help, depending on the core cause(s) of overeating. Some people might encounter subconscious resistance not explained above, and may need a private session with a hypnotherapist who is trained to guide the subconscious back to the event(s) that initially caused the problem. Nonetheless, the script may help whether or not the user invests in private sessions.

Weight Reduction Script

(Use one of the deepeners from Chapter 5 at the beginning of this script)

Life is made up of moments, and at this very moment, you are very, very focused, on looking slim, and healthy. And it will be the same in the next moment, and the next hour. And the hours will turn into days, and the days into weeks, and you will feel proud of yourself, for now, you are deeply, deeply relaxed. You only eat, when you are hungry, and you eat very slowly, so very, very slowly, savoring the taste, enjoying each and every mouthful, because now, your relationship with food has changed, and you are deeply relaxed whenever you are in the presence of food. Now you listen carefully, for the signal from your stomach that says to you, "I am no longer hungry." You do not wait until you are full, because by then, you have already overeaten. When picking food to eat, you are choosing the food you enjoy, and not the food you think you should be eating. You eat what you want, but only when you are hungry. Food has become your friend, and you stop eating just as soon as you are no longer hungry. It may be just two or three bites, but as soon as satisfaction replaces your hunger, you stop. Relaxing deeper, and deeper now, just let go, completely. You accept yourself, and love yourself, and all the wonderful changes that are occurring inside you, changes which you are aware of, and other changes which are now happening at a deeper level. You crave water, and water is the only thing you truly crave for. Cool, pure, refreshing water, is the now only thing, you truly long for. You enjoy light exercise, and are now making a solid effort, to get out each day (Pause). Whenever you get a feeling, you deal with that feeling in the appropriate way. If you feel lonely, you ring a friend. If you are bored, you get up and get active. There is no amount of food that could ever satisfy a feeling, or an emotion. You have tried to feed the feeling before, and it has not worked, at best, it may have been a temporary distraction, but then the feeling came back, and there was more food, and more feelings, and so you got into vicious cycle. Well the past, is truly the past, and now you find it easy, to deal with your feelings without food. Your subconscious mind understands that you wish to speed up your metabolism. This is because of the images you are passing down to it, images of someone who is thin. Now it is speeding up your metabolism, faster and faster, faster and faster. You are finding it easy to stay strong, and you are sticking to the rules. This is serious business, and you are extremely focused on the task at hand. For the next while I will remain silent. I want you to let your mind do its work now, all by itself. Now it is making these suggestions a permanent part of your thinking.

Chapter 16

Self-Hypnosis for Allergies, Skin Disorders and Stuttering

"That which is foreign to the mind and body, creates both realistic and unrealistic fear."
Cathal O'Briain

About Allergies and Allergens

Allergies are the body's way of protecting a person from what it perceives as a life-threatening substance (allergen). The parts of the body that are prone to react to allergies include the eyes, nose, skin, lungs and stomach. Allergic reactions can range from having itchy eyes to breaking out in hives.

Allergens are basically substances that are foreign to the body and cause allergic reactions. During an allergic response, the body produces *histamine* in an effort to protect itself; but all too often the brain simply makes a mistake. This over-reaction of your immune system, in an effort to fight off what it perceives to be a threat, may cause you to sneeze or breathe incorrectly. Self-hypnosis rectifies this mistake by creating a new reaction to the allergenic substances. Once the subconscious understands that particular substances are not life-threatening, it then stops producing histamines unnecessarily when in contact with them. This is when the allergy usually disappears.

You can release an allergic reaction or set of reactions within a short space of time by using trance methods; but there really is no textbook formula for treating allergies in a general manner. This is due to the fact that there are a large variety of allergies out there. Because people suffer in such uniquely different ways, you may have to attempt a number of strategies before finding the one that works best for you.

Allergies respond particularly well to the placebo effect. If your subconscious has been convinced that an inhaler filled with water is medicinal, the end result may possibly be the disappearance of asthma. This is because your mind switches off an allergic reaction once it knows that you are safe within your surrounding environment.

Allergens that have the potential to create an allergic reaction include: pollen, grass, dust mites, cats, dogs, feathers, milk, eggs, wheat, peanuts, bee and wasp stings, mould and fungi, household chemicals, drugs and medicines, along with many others. The symptoms that result from exposure to allergens depend largely on the route of entry taken and the amount of exposure to the allergens. The chemical structure of an allergen ultimately defines the route it takes; for example, dust-mites may have little effect upon the skin but can seriously affect breathing; when allergens are swallowed they often make their way to parts of the body far from the point of entry. This can cause symptoms to occur that sometimes appear new and unrelated to the allergy.

Allergic reactions range from *mild* to *severe*. In a severe reaction, known as *anaphylaxis* or *anaphylactic shock*, there is a decrease in blood pressure caused by dilation of the blood vessels. Severe reactions sometimes follow mild reactions. A person could suffer low blood pressure after experience itching and sneezing. This type of reaction should be treated as an emergency and immediate medical attention is necessary.

Allergies can develop at any age or time, even while you are in the womb. They are common in children but may give rise to symptoms for the first time in adulthood. Although you may inherit the tendency to develop allergies from your parents, you may never actually suffer the same symptoms. When an allergy develops in adulthood, there may be psychological problems in need of address.

The Psychological Forces Behind Allergies

There are often *psychosomatic forces* at work behind an allergy. Even if the mind is not responsible for an allergy formation, the potential for it causing or exacerbating further allergic reactions is nearly always present. Your emotional state can help or worsen allergic symptoms. High stress levels affect the body's natural ability to fight allergens. So, by lowering your stress levels in trance, you also bolster your immune and belief system. This makes you less prone to the effects of allergens because now you have re-aligned your emotions so that they can work effectively for you again. While self-hypnosis helps most allergic conditions, some require professional medical treatment. Please ensure you get a diagnosis before using self-hypnosis to treat your allergy.

Gaining Relief from Allergies

During a hypnotic session, give your subconscious the following suggestions and repeat them a few times. Use your imagination, but more importantly put belief and expectation behind them:

> *"My immune system is growing stronger and stronger. It reacts appropriately every time I come in contact with allergens. It always reacts appropriately."*
>
> *"My body is generating new ways to fight hay fever."*
>
> *"There is a protective shield around me now. A bright yellow force field surrounds my entire body. It protects me from allergens. Nothing can penetrate this powerful shield. It is strong and present at all times."*

(If you have a pollen allergy, imagine pollen deflecting away from the shield, back into the environment.)

> *"My body is fighting allergens as a whole unit."*

(Often when we think about our particular allergy or symptom we tend to focus on the areas of entry. If we imagine our entire body fighting allergies as a single unit, this draws attention away from the areas most affected and bolsters our overall capacity to deal with allergens effectively.)

"Energy is moving from my mind to the route of entry. This area is filled with and protected by healing energy. Nothing can affect it or travel into it."

Other Ways to Combat Allergies

There are many alternative approaches to the treatment of allergies. Eating fish increases your intake of Omega-3 fatty acids, which are useful in combating allergies. Fruit and vegetables with high levels of antioxidants are also beneficial, especially citrus fruit. The antioxidants create a natural antihistamine action and help protect the body by bolstering our defense mechanisms. Here are some other useful ways to combat allergies:

Reduce intake of dairy products.

Cut down on processed food. Eat fresh.

Cut down on refined sugar and white flour. This reduces the toxin load on your immune system.

Increase your vitamin C intake. It acts as a natural antihistamine.

Put a drop of lavender oil with one teaspoon of carrier oil and rub it into your sinus area. The helps prevent hay fever and other allergies.

There are special covers you can buy for your pillowcases and mattresses that help reduce exposure to dust mites. They may prove useful at nighttime.

Wash your bed clothes at least once a fortnight.

Use a dehumidifier to keep humidity in your house below fifty per cent.

Clean or replace any air vents, and fit with a vent filter if necessary.

Vacuum regularly.

The more clutter you have, the more dust you have. Avoid shelves, big light shades, pictures and so on.

About Skin Disorders

People often compare the skin to a mirror of the self. Imbalance within the nervous system is often reflected in the condition of your skin. Psychosomatic forces may trigger responses or exacerbate already existing ones. Therefore it is important to work with causation, symptom and reaction when dealing with skin disorders. You must find out which of the above relates to you, in other words, which one is most likely to trigger a negative response.

The symptoms of most skin disorders are usually not constant, which illustrates that you have an ability to switch off from symptoms. Simply involving yourself in things that make you happy can cause a symptom to disappear. But thinking thoughts of a fearful nature may cause the symptom to reappear. The unconscious controls this on and off switch mechanism, and can become habitual over time. But you can unlearn this habit by using hypnosis. When you change your subconscious attitude towards particular objects, actions or situations in trance, you also change your reactions, reflexes and responses to them in reality.

A reaction such as a rash may compound a person's inability to seek help. This is often due to their problem being visible to the onlooker, making it harder to get support from family, friends, GPs or therapists. From time to time people can literally get under your skin. This is why it's necessary to mentally protect yourself in the presence of those who bring out the worst in you. The rash may be a way for your subconscious to move you quickly away from a person or situation you unconsciously fear. So it's down to you to convince it otherwise. You are the one in full control. You dictate how you wish to feel and behave. By breathing deeply and repeating affirmations of control, you can remain in command of your body's physiological reactions. Once again your mind has learned that there is really nothing to fear from objects, people, situations or environments.

The Effects of Stress on Your Skin

Stress increases the vulnerability of the nervous system and this has a direct effect on your skin. The more you are stressed, the more your nervous system reacts in response to stress by creating a reaction. Using self-hypnosis as a means to relieve stress can significantly reduce your negative reactions. It's also another vital part of regaining control of autonomic functions such as breathing and heart rate. By reducing stress, you reduce symptoms. And by regaining control over your autonomic system you put yourself back in charge of your physiological functions.

Using Imagery to Heal Your Skin

Some skin conditions respond very well to being exposed to ultra violet light. In self-hypnosis you can create imagery that has a similar effect to UV light. By imagining the sun is safely shining down on you, mental exposure to its healing rays can have a positive healing effect upon the skin. Alternatively, you can visualize yourself getting into a warm bath of healing water, feeling the water touching your toes first, then your feet and legs, the way you would normally step into a bath. A spiritual person may imagine God intervening and blessing the water, making it pure and giving it the ability to heal your skin.

The idea is to render up images of your skin in perfect condition as much as possible. By doing this, you are re-programming your subconscious to fulfill what it understands is your desire. Imagine that you are looking in a mirror. Notice how your skin is beginning to clear up. Focus your attention upon the desired result and think no more about the feared reaction.

"Everyday in every way my skin is getting better and better." This type of suggestion spurs the imagination and can be repeated

while looking in the mirror.

If your skin condition started at a certain age, a useful technique is to regress yourself back in time and see your skin as it was before the condition started. By associating in the present how your skin felt back then, your subconscious can revert back to a once used program, thus making your physiological responses the same again.

Using Imagery to Heal Warts, Psoriasis, and Eczema

Common warts are a virus that can remain on the skin for unpredictable lengths of time. For many people they disappear during the transition from child to teenager or from teenager to adult. You may choose from a variety of procedures for treating warts. Freezing the wart with liquid nitrogen is one popular way. Another involves the application of acid on a regular basis. As a last resort some people get them surgically removed. But even then, there is always the risk of a new wart growing back in the same spot or different location. All of us have the capacity to fight wart-causing viruses, but simply haven't learned how to direct our healing power. The subconscious must know that you want rid of warts and also that you trust in its ability to eliminate them.

"I trust in my subconscious to eliminate these warts."

Warts are highly susceptible to changes in blood flow. Imagery is often effective with hypnosis to change blood flow in the body. Just imagine sitting in front of an open fire and warming your hands over it. Involve the senses and really feel the heat in your hands, as they get hotter and hotter. Or imagine holding a mug of hot tea with your hands tightly around it. By actively visualizing this in hypnosis the brain will begin dilating the blood vessels in the hand in response to the heat.

Those with *psoriasis* or *eczema* should also use imagery that affects skin temperature. Imagining the sun's warm rays on your skin will increase your skin's temperature and alter the blood flow to the skin. This will help your skin to dry out, thus improving your skin's condition. Psoriasis seems to get better in the summertime and worse in the winter, but the good news is, changing seasons does not interfere with self-hypnosis. Whenever there's no sun in the sky or the availability of a sun bed, use hypnosis to recreate its effect in your mind.

Psoriasis and eczema can be irritating and extremely painful at times. In milder cases of eczema the skin becomes dry, flaky, hot and itchy. In more severe cases it can get broken, raw and bleed. The causes of eczema are difficult to identify, but, as always, psychological forces are more than likely attributing to the maintenance and agitation of the symptom, thus making it difficult to overcome through purely medicinal means. A traumatic experience may trigger the beginning of a skin disorder such as eczema. A shock to the system can cause your body to manifest the disease, as eczema is often an outward expression of an internal crisis.

Outbreaks of psoriasis and eczema will happen through times of increased stress. Financial difficulty, dry humid conditions, pollen, dust-mites, certain foods, drinks and preservatives, contact with yeast, tobacco, detergent, and even blood circulation can bring it on. As with allergies, the immune system sees the stimulus as a threat and produces an unnecessary response in the skin such as shedding or flaking. Hypnosis can alter this response by using a protective shield or imaginary pane of glass to gradually expose yourself to the stimuli that aggravates your skin. By using such techniques, over time your immune system eventually stops overreacting.

Using Glove Anesthesia to Stop Itching and Scratching

Here is a good technique for altering your perception to sensitivity. It involves numbing your hand through the use of imagery, in order to gain relief from itchy areas that tend to be scratched more than others. It may take a few goes to get right, but is worth the practice as it can be used to help a range of problems.

> *On getting yourself nice and relaxed into hypnosis, imagine placing your hand into a bucket of ice cold water.*
>
> *Involve your senses and clearly imagine the coldness of the icy water as it now begins to numb your hand. Getting colder and colder, freezing cold water, numbing your hand until it's as cold as an icicle, frozen solid and completely numb.*
>
> *When you are satisfied it's numb, take your hand out of the icy water and move it to the area of most discomfort, where the scratching can get bad.*
>
> *Lay your hand upon this area and feel the numbness transferring from your hand into the itchy region. Feel it getting numb until there is no sensitivity there at all, until you can feel absolutely nothing.*
>
> *When you finish this, continue to work on the other areas of the body in the same way.*
>
> *Whenever you want, imagine returning to the bucket and regenerating the analgesia in your hand by placing it back into the freezing water.*

Skin Healing Script

(Use one of the deepeners from Chapter 5 at the beginning of this script)

With each day that passes, you are getting better, and better, and your skin, is looking clearer now, so much clearer now. And you are happier, more content, and more self-assured. Relaxing in trance is helping your skin to heal at a very deep level. This outward affect upon your skin, protects and nourishes it. And while your skin is being protected, and nourished, your imagination is also creating new ways for you to heal. Your creative imagination, is now rendering up images of you looking fit, and healthy, eating the right food, getting fresh air into your lungs. For in these powerful, colorful images, your skin is completely healed, totally clear, and perfect in every way. From the tips of your toes, to the top of your head. I want you to imagine now, that you are sitting on a rock, right in the center of a warm lagoon. You are surrounded by a warm tropical mist, created by a waterfall rushing near to you. And here in place of healing, you touch the water with both hands, and can feel it around your waist. Your legs are completely submerged, and the upper half of your body is exposed to the warm mist, and cleansing air. And while you sit, and listen, to the calm, relaxing sounds of the rainforest, you gently splash the healing water over your body, and it feels warm, and soothing. And so you gently splash the healing water over your body, warm and pure, and with the power to heal and change, leaving your skin looking as good as the day you were born. And in your own time now, I want you to stand up, and begin walking slowly towards the waterfall. And while you draw closer to the waterfall, you can feel the mist, spraying harder upon your body. But now you are safe, and secure, and your desire is to feel the waterfall crashing over your body; you want to know what true healing feels like. And now you are standing just a foot away, almost there now (Pause). Just take that step now. Take the step and feel the water crashing down on your head, your shoulders, and now your back, and legs. Feel its healing power covering every inch of your body with force, and feel the light of the sun bursting through gaps in the waterfall, healing your skin with its healing light. Water and light, light and water, covering your body from top to bottom, soothing your skin. Making it as pure as the water, as pure as the light, as pure as the water, as pure as the light, all the while you drift deeper, and deeper, drifting down, down, deeper and deeper (pause for 10 minutes). And now you have bathed in the healing water, come back out, and dry off in the sun by the edge of the forest. And the next time you come here, you will go much deeper into relaxation, ten times deeper, because this is your safe place, the place where you go very deeply into relaxation, and comfort. For the next few moments I will remain silent. I want you to let these important suggestions I've just given you, sink very deeply now. Now your subconscious is making these important suggestions a permanent part of your thinking.

About Stuttering and Stammering

Stuttering and stammering are a complex set of behaviors that mostly involve repeating words and sounds, prolonging sounds, hesitation and avoiding or substituting certain words for others. There are many types of stutters, including developmental stuttering, *psychogenic* and *neurogenic* stuttering. *Developmental* stuttering usually occurs because a child's neurological system is not ready for all the language they are trying to say. Neurogenic stuttering is a signal problem between the brain and the nerves or muscles controlling speech. Neurogenic stuttering has repetitions, blocks and prolongations. Psychogenic stuttering originates in the area of the brain that directs thought and reasoning and is a rare type of stutter.

Self-hypnosis is a useful tool for helping stuttering and stammering because it gives the user control and confidence, two things often lacking due to the embarrassment that accompanies the problem. Breathing deeply and diaphragmatically is central to the self-hypnotic procedure. As a single entity it produces significant relaxation in the mouth, cheeks, jaw, tongue and throat regions, as well as the rest of the body. Spot-checking breathing throughout the day helps the stutterer to maintain a relaxed face, especially during times of increased stress. Using guided imagery in hypnosis to implant pictures of full control and relaxation helps the self-image to become enhanced. One can visualize themselves addressing a group of people, focusing attention on a smooth, rhythmic delivery. Post-hypnotic suggestions and cues are given in hypnosis to create positive trigger responses to affect speech and its timing; for example, *"Whenever I tap my foot, my voice automatically follows its rhythm."* or

"Whenever a question is asked of me, my face becomes relaxed and my answer is delivered clearly."

Ways to Help Overcome Stuttering and Stammering

Whenever you are on your own, have a metronome present. Set it at 65 to 70 beats per minute (the beat of a resting heart). Listen to it both consciously in the backround. This will instill the beat in your mind. Use the metronome to guide your mind into trance. Fix your eyes upon it and concentrate using both visual and auditory senses. Think only of your breath and the beat. After you close your eyes, continue listening attentively, using the rhythmic sound of the metronome as your deepener. Use suggestion to deepen if you wish, but make sure to time your suggestions to the beat; for example, *"Tic, tic, deeper, tic, tic, and deeper, tic, tic, deeper, tic, tic, and deeper, tic, tic, etc."*

The beat must influence your thoughts, suggestions and images. After spending some time relaxing in trance, start saying the lyrics of your favourite song aloud. Let your speech flow with the rhythm, and make variations to your time, but always to the beat. Allow the momentum that carries you along to become instilled in your subconscious. The beat must become an instinctive part of you, commanding your speech intuitively, so give your mind suggestions such as, *"This beat is forever inside of me. I can turn it up and I can turn it down. It's constant rhythm is resonating in my mind, body and soul."*

The images you implant must also possess rhythm. Feel the beat within your imagination and project it into bright, colourful images of you looking confident and in full control. In control of your breathing, your words, your posture and your mindset. Feel how relaxed your jaw is in hypnosis and say, *"My jaw feels so relaxed now. It always feels relaxed, day and night, night and day."*

Notice how deep and steady your breathing is and say, *"My breathing is deep and smooth, and everytime I speak, I relax even deeper."*

The following script may provide varying degrees of help, depending on the core cause(s) of stuttering. Some people who stutter might need a private session with a hypnotherapist who is trained in regression therapy, in order to guide the subconscious back to the event(s) that initially caused the problem. Nonetheless, the script may help whether or not the user invests in a private session.

Stuttering Script

(Use a deepener from Chapter 5 and have a metronome ticking in the background)

And in this beautiful, quiet state of calmness, your subconscious is focused upon the sound of my voice, and the metronome. The beat of the metronome, as it ticks away gently in the background, is resonating deep within your mind, deeper and deeper, the beat, the rhythm, penetrating your subconscious, becoming a permanent part of you, the beat, the rhythm, so just listen to it now (Pause for 2 minutes). And when you speak, you speak to the beat, and when you talk, you talk to the rhythm, to the beat, to the rhythm, all the while you relax deeper and deeper, going deeper and deeper, drifting further and further, further and further, drifting down, down, down, all the way now, and with every breath that you take, you are moving deeper into calm, deeper into peace, and deeper into tranquility. And the sound of the beat, is now a part of you, instilled in you forever, its rhythm, creating perfect flow in speech, and a smooth delivery in speech, so easily, and effortlessly, easily, and naturally, to the beat, the beat, so listen, listen, listen to it now (Pause for 2 minutes). I want you to repeat after me:

"The beat that I hear, while I speak loud and clear, reminds me to speak, to the sound of the beat (Pause for sentence)."

And once again, repeat after me:

"The beat that I hear, while I speak loud and clear, reminds me to speak, to the sound of the beat (pause for sentence)."

Now I want you to say the words of your favorite song or poem. Just say the words of your favorite poem or song, to the beat, to the rhythm (Pause for song or poem). And the way you speak now, flowing perfectly to the beat, is how you speak permanently, forever to the beat, forever to the rhythm. You talk with clarity, smoothly and easily, as the words just flow off your tongue, in a calm and relaxing manner. Your jaw is loose and limp, and your confidence is growing each and every time you converse with those around you. And the more you speak, the more you relax, and the more you relax, the better you speak. Speaking clearly and smoothly, as each word flows to the rhythm, as each word flows to the beat. You enjoy talking, and speaking your mind with confidence, for every time you speak, you do so to the rhythm, to the beat, to the rhythm, to the beat. Allow these important suggestions to become a permanent part of your thinking. Just let your subconscious mind do its work now, all by itself.

Chapter 17

Self-Hypnosis for Pain Control

"Pain comes in many forms; all of which are painful, all of which are controllable."
Cathal O'Briain

Using Trance to Control Pain

The purpose of most pain is to provide a warning signal indicating there is something wrong in the body. Once you discover the source of your pain, it is then no longer necessary for you to experience it. However, you must find out the core cause of your pain before using self-hypnosis to reduce or eliminate it altogether. Much research carried out over the years proves that hypnosis is an effective tool in preventing and alleviating almost every type of pain. However, from an early age, and through no fault of our own, most people learn to fear and endure pain, rather than how to acknowledge and control it. Over-reactions from concerned parents, the sight of blood, the noise of other children crying when they are hurt, can all encourage a developing mind to react inappropriately to pain. Our psychological conditioning greatly affects our natural response to pain. But this doesn't necessarily mean that we cannot alter our responses. Self-hypnosis is one such way to change your responses. For when the mind and body are as one in a state of total hypnotic relaxation, there simply is no pain.

With hypnosis, your pain threshold is much higher. So whether you suffer from occasional migraine or severe arthritis, deep relaxation is one of the most natural and effective ways to control pain without the need for drugs. We should never suggest the direct removal of pain to the subconscious, but only its reduction. Pain is real, and is there for a reason. Charles Tebbetts taught his hypnotherapy students that pain is a warning that something is wrong with the body, so the cause must be diagnosed by someone qualified to do so (Hunter, 2000). Removing it without first understanding why it's there could result in a serious injury or possibly worse. Pain is a personal, subjective experience. By learning to respect its value, you learn to remove its ability to linger on.

Hypnosis can turn a sharp pain into a feeling of warmth. Using imagery, you can change the color of pain from red to blue, or into any other color you find soothing to your senses. We can visualize pins and needles as cotton wool, and feel daggering pains as relaxing ripples. You may desensitize the images that drive your fear by turning what you normally would imagine and associate with pain, into its exact opposite. Dark becomes light, pointed becomes round, sore becomes soothing, stiff become loose, and so on. By changing your mental images, you change your response. And by changing your response, you control pain.

The Three Phases in Pain Relief

Hypnosis for pain relief works in three phases. The first is complete physical relaxation. When people are in pain, muscles become tense and exacerbate pain. Hypnosis brings about the level of relaxation required for total muscular relaxation. The second phase is sensory alteration. Transforming pain into another sensation causes a different perception of the pain in the mind. The third phase is through mental diversion or distraction. This is when attention is drawn away from the source of pain, thus severing the connection between fear in the mind and symptom in the body.

If someone receives emotional gains as a result of their pains, this can help maintain or worsen existing symptoms. The pain may actually provide a means of getting more love and attention from family and friends. For some it can be a way of avoiding work. A person may experience stomach problems when thinking about going to social event they feel uncomfortable with. It isn't pain that stops them, but more an issue of self-confidence. Arthritis and back pain act up in the cold, but they also act up when your body is under stress. At times, pain can be an attempt by your subconscious to move you away from a situation it feels you are unable to handle. So it's up to you to inform your subconscious through suggestion and imagery that you fear nothing, and this is best done in trance. Here are some of the types of suggestion you can implant:

Suggestions to Reduce Pain

"Every day, in every way, I'm getting better and better."

"There's that nice rippling sensation in my shoulder again. It's a pleasant sensation, warm and soothing, warm and soothing."

(For burns)

"It feels like cool, blue water, running through my veins, soothing my skin, healing my skin. This healing is being accelerated, and I am healing faster and faster."

(For toothache)

"My hand is in a bucket off ice water, and it is getting colder and colder, the water is freezing, unbearably cold. By touching my face, I am transferring the numbness in my hand to my tooth. As a result my whole mouth is completely numb."

(Glove Anesthesia is used for any part of the body)

Induction No. 9: Pain Control

Sit down on a chair and begin to breathe deeply.

Focus your eyes upon a point in the room and think only of your breath while you stare.

When you find yourself slipping into a light trance with your eyes open, focus your attention upon a point on your body that feels good and pain-free. If you have a pain in your left knee, focus on the right one. The same goes for your hand or foot. Concentrate and breathe; focus your attention.

While you stare at your good knee, think about how well it's functioning. Imagine the way the blood circulates freely through it, and how the healthy muscles and tendons make it work so well. Continue to breathe very deeply and focus your mind intently upon the good knee.

Now switch your attention to the bad knee. Rate the level of pain in your bad knee on a scale of 1-10; 10 being severe pain and 1 being no pain at all. Now imagine the sensation in your knee changing from sharp to soft, from fire to liquid, hot to cold, or whatever works for you creatively. The idea is to use your imagination to change the sensation you presently feel into its exact opposite. Keep focused and breathe.

Return back to the good knee and think about how healthy it feels again. Focus intently upon it, exploring its anatomy in your mind, thinking about how well it functions as a bodily mechanism.

Now switch back again to the bad knee and rate it again on a scale of 1-10. Even if it feels as though the pain has not yet reduced, drop the scale of your pain down by one or two numbers, such as from 10 to 9 or 8. By reducing the numbers in your mind, you reduce the pain in your body. If you have difficulty visualizing the scale, imagine that you feel yourself turning a dial that lowers the scale and reduces the pain.

Return back to the good knee and think about how good it feels again. Keep repeating this sequence of lowering the numbers on the scale until you reach an acceptable level of comfort; 9, 8, 7... moving down the scale, reducing the level of discomfort each time you drop down a figure.

Now give yourself some post-hypnotic suggestions, for example:

"My knee feels good. When I'm out walking, it is strong, so very, very strong."

"Whenever I get that warm, rippling sensation, I automatically begin to breathe deeply and relax."

Induction No. 10: Headache and Migraine

If you feel a migraine coming on, relax using hypnosis and visualize your hands getting hotter and hotter. Migraines are thought to be associated with the dilation of blood vessels in the brain. By imagining your hands are getting hotter, you help blood to flow from the brain to the extremities. This enables coronary arteries to return to normal, thus reducing pain. Think of a fire or a bucket of hot water to generate this sensation of heat in your hands.

Roy Hunter, referred to previously in this book, used a different technique to effectively deal with his migraines. After suffering with them from childhood through his late thirties, he would use self-hypnosis to go to his peaceful place and then imagine a coolness around his head. According to Hunter, this helped reduce the frequency to less than 10 per cent of his previous history, and he reduced the severity of the occasional headaches to only a fraction of previous severity. He claims that stress can make him backslide if he doesn't get to his peaceful place (in imagination) quick enough when his buttons get pushed. The lesson here is that stress can intensify headaches somewhat quickly; so if you suffer from headaches, you may benefit greatly by using hypnosis to deal with stress.

Case History 3: Fibromayalgia

Client C, a fifty two year old man, came to me in a lot of pain due to an upsurge in his fibromayalgia. At times it would cripple him to the point of tears. What bothered him the most was the fact that his condition started forcing him to take half-days off work. On several occasions, due to an intense stabbing pain in his left ankle, he had to leave his car at work and take the bus home. He described the journey on the bus as a nightmare, with people giving him strange looks every time he jolted in response to a sudden attack of pain. The unpleasant symptoms that accompanied his condition became an embarrassment, because as well as occuring at the worst possible moments, they were now also generating a state of panic in his mind and body. This would make him sweat profusley, and cause his heart to race faster than normal. He felt as though he was at breaking point, and it showed on his face.

He responded well to hypnosis and felt little or no pain throughout the procedure. On returning him to full awareness, I spent some time teaching him self-hypnosis so that he too could learn to achieve this relaxed pain-free state. Then I asked him to decribe in detail what his pain felt like on a typical day. He described a constant, throbbing, hot pain that would begin in his left foot and then work its way into his ankle. From there it would move through his leg, until eventually his entire leg region, as far as his hip, would throb with pain. On a bad day it felt like somebody was stabbing him in the ankle and knee with a knife. I got him to close his eyes and then asked him to tell me where he presently felt pain in his body. He told me that he was pretty much pain-free, except for a hot, throbbing sensation in his left ankle.

Then I asked, "What color or colors do you see in your imagination when you think of the sensation in your ankle?"

To which he responded, "I see red."

"Why red?" I asked him.

"Because it's like a red hot, burning sensation."

I asked him to open his eyes and focus his attention upon his ankle. Then I said, "While you are focusing, I want you to use your imagination. I want you to imagine the hot color red in your ankle, turning into a cool, soothing blue. Red becoming blue, hot becoming cold, and flames becoming water."

I then asked him to rate the cool, blue sensation in his ankle on a scale of 1-10, 10 being severe pain and 1 being mild or practically non-existant. He rated it on the scale as 7. Then I asked him to switch his attention to his right ankle, and focus intently upon it while breathing slowly and deeply.

"How does your right ankle feel?" I asked him.

"It feels fine."

Then I asked him to think about how good his right ankle felt; to visualize the bone, the muscle, the sinews, the blood and how it functioned in general as a body part. After doing this for roughly a minute, I got him to switch his attention back to his left ankle. I asked him to tell me where he rated the cool, blue sensation now on the scale of 1-10. He told me that he experienced significant improvement and he was now at about 5. I asked him to return to the right knee, and got him to think about how good it felt for a minute, before switching back to the left knee and rating it once again. This time he rated it as 4, and so, my client kept on repeating this sequence until eventually he was able to rate the pain as 1 on the scale. Through using self-hypnosis with his eyes open, he managed to control his pain through mind power alone. This gave my client much hope for the future, because now he had a drug-free way of controling pain before it had a chance to escalate to the point of agony and panic.

A week later he reported back to me. He told me he was able to put his mind to the test the very next day after his first hypnotherapy session. He was at work, helping a colleague to shift office equipment, which involved carrying heavy boxes and much bending down. At about twelve noon his left foot started to feel its usual hot throbbing pain. He took ten minutes out and found a quiet room in the office to practice self-hypnosis. First he got in control of his breathing, and then went through the procedure he learned a day earlier. After a short time he had managed to sever the connection between fear and symptom. On returning to work, he was able to maintain control of his pain for the rest of the afternoon. He found that releasing air very slowly through pursed lips was a good form of distraction and diversion from pain, while helping him to relax and achieve clarity of mind at the same time. By learning to control his responses, particuarly in work, my client's confidence grew rapidly in the months that followed. He accepted that he would probably have to use self-hypnosis for the rest of his life in order to keep pain at bay. But because my client was a patient and focused individual, I could see that he was willing to do whatever was necessary to stop fibromayalgia being in control of him. Panic attacks became a thing of the past and his perception of pain changed completely. Rippling warmth replaced stabbing pain, and sharp became smooth in his vocabulary of words. By cleaning up his internal language, my client was able to alter his response to pain by productively using his imagination. This simple yet effective use of self-hypnosis literally gave my client a new lease of life.

Controlling Pain During Labor and Childbirth

For some expectant women the thought of labor is enough to create agonizing images of pain, sweat and tears. But for those who do not fearfully anticipate the powerful force that will soon take over their body, using self-hypnosis to eliminate pain, stress and fear, has proven to be natural, safe and better for baby too. When giving birth, it is possible to change the sensation of pain to pressure. The more relaxed a mother-to-be is, the easier, faster, and less complicated labor and birth become. Some mothers become so relaxed, they find it almost impossible to identify when exactly they are having a contraction. Through self-hypnosis they turn pain into pressure. When the mother's body is this relaxed, the baby just flows out and sometimes after just a few pushes.

From the moment a woman realizes she is pregnant, preparation for the big day using relaxation techniques and positive imagery should be used to remove fear. We should see the process of giving birth as a happy and wondrous event, eagerly anticipated. But many cultures tend to view it as something to be feared because of the pain they associate with it. This expectation of fear and pain is what makes labor so difficult. If a girl grows up believing that childbirth is a comfortable and joyous experience, providing she doesn't hear otherwise, she should remain free of fear, tension and pain when her time comes to give birth. By reprogramming your mind to expect relaxation and pressure, instead of fear and pain, less adrenaline is produced. Adrenaline is one of the main reasons why labor normally becomes dysfunctional. There is less chance of needing a *cesarean section* during a natural, *hypno-birth*.

The woman using self-hypnosis during birth trains her mind to produce anasthesia when and where it's needed. The feeling of building pressure is used as a cue to relax even deeper. So as labor progresses, instead of it painfully intensifying, the buildup and pressure now create a sense of relaxation in the mind and body. When the body is instructed to flow harmoniously along with the birth process, this opens up and releases tightness and tension. It also helps the downward movement to work easily and effectively, resulting in a shorter birth. By reducing the amount of trauma to the baby during the birth process, the baby is more likely to be happier and more relaxed.

The Benefits of Using Hypnosis During Labor and Childbirth

Hypnosis shortens labor time and the second stage of labor. This is because it minimizes the resistance of the muscles used in birth as a response to pain and stress.

Hypnosis enhances comfort and sleep during and after pregnancy.

Hypnosis helps control nausea and vomiting.

Hypnosis helps to stop post-partum depression beginning.

Hypnosis creates a stronger bond between mother and baby.

Hypnosis creates a peaceful birthing environment.

Hypnosis may reduce the need for episiotomies and anesthesia.

Hypnosis helps to remove negative beliefs about the labor process.

Hypnosis helps adjust blood pressure naturally.

Hypnosis increases the mother's confidence in her own ability to give birth naturally, putting her in control of herself, while at the same time letting nature do its job in a proficient manner.

Hypnosis helps to create the level of relaxation needed to stop the flow of catecholamines, the stress hormone released during labor. Catecholamines make it difficult for the circular muscles of the uterus to relax, causing the uterus muscles to work hard, creating longer, harder contractions. Catecholamine release is a fear-based response that creates constriction in the muscles. Self hypnosis turns off catecholamines and switches on endorphins.

The experience of pain in childbirth is the result of an unnatural process of fear. Fear produces tension, which then creates tightness and clamping of the muscles. Tension works in opposition to the body giving birth. Self-hypnosis removes the fear, which removes tension, which removes tightness and clamping. The end result is pressure, not pain.

Fewer drugs or no drugs at all mean less risk of side effects for mother and baby. Birth is then completely natural; the way nature intended it to be.

There are fewer interventions and complications during labor.

There is a time distortion with hypnosis. This makes labor time feel much shorter than it actually is.

With hypnosis there is less shock to the system and a quicker recovery.

Because hypnosis helps with the second and active stage of labor, including the delivery of the baby, there is less need for operational delivery. Complete anesthesia of the perineum eases delivery, episiotomy and suturing of the perineum.

There are many good hypno-birthing courses out there for expectant women who wish to use self-hypnosis for childbirth. This book has all the tools you need, but getting out there and becoming more involved with others can be fun. If you have a partner, husband or close friend, they too can learn and may even take on the role of hypnotherapist, before, during and after birth. As always, breath, suggestion and imagination all play their part in childbirth, but so too does freedom from fear.

Childbirth Preparation Script

(Use one of the deepeners from Chapter 5 at the beginning of this script)

And now while you are completely relaxed, I want you to imagine that your body is getting lighter, and lighter. Your body, is now becoming lighter, as light as a feather, and you are beginning to float, going higher, and higher. And while you are floating higher, you feel safe, and secure, and inside your womb, it feels safe, and secure, as you just continue to float, and drift, drift and float, going higher, and higher. Softly and gently, like a feather on the breeze, drifting and floating, going higher, and higher (Pause). And while you drift along, ripples of relaxation are generating in your feet, rippling from the soles of your feet, upward, into your legs. And this pleasant relaxation, is now spreading up to your thighs and waist (Pause). And now it is moving from the base of your spine, all the way to the top, and into your neck. Waves of relaxation, rippling through your body now, caressing each and every cell and fiber of your being. From the tips of your toes, all the way to the top of your head, waves of relaxation, reaching and stretching out to every part. And the more you breathe, the more you relax, and the more you relax, the better you feel. Relaxing deeper, and deeper still, just letting go, completely. The life you hold inside you, fills your womb with a sense of peace and unconditional love. And every breath that you take, relaxes your womb, and baby too. For you are in control of your body, all the time, savoring each day that brings you a step closer to having your baby. Your body knows exactly what it's doing, and you trust in your mind's ability to guide you through a relaxing, a joyous childbirth. And in the same way you are deeply relaxed now, so too are you deeply relaxed giving birth. You are aware of the pressure you feel when giving birth, because you are imagining it right now, a pressure that is necessary to move baby along the birth canal easily, and comfortably. You are aware of this force, and how it feels, and you are looking forward now to feeling this force inside you, doing its work, and to the natural rhythm of your body. And you are full of energy at the moment. Surrounding your body is a strong, vibrant energy field, and this is what makes you glow. I want you to feel this energy, vibrating on the top of your skin, a sort of pleasant, tingling sensation (Pause). And now I want you to feel this energy, protecting your womb, like a force field (Pause). And the more you relax, the more you vibrate, and the more you vibrate, the brighter you glow, drifting deeper, and deeper still, just letting go, completely. The energy that surrounds your body is created by your subconscious mind, and because your mind is now happy and focused, it is providing you with as much energy as you need, with extra reserves in stock for whenever you need them. And because your diet is natural and healthy, so too is your developing baby. You have healthy food choices, because you know what's best for you both. Expecting a healthy child and a relaxing birth has given you so much confidence, because now you know that you are going to be the best mother in the world, and that you have the necessary skills and resources within you to make childbirth an enjoyable experience, where you just slip easily into hypnosis (Pause). You slip so easily into hypnosis giving birth, and you always remember to breathe out slowly, and completely, breathing through pursed lips. And every contraction serves to relax you further and further, deeper and deeper, and if you happen to notice a contraction, it automatically sends you ten times deeper into trance, ten times deeper. You are influenced by your own thoughts and desires. The instinctive mother knows what is right for her developing baby. She has insight and intuition guiding her every move, and her reactions are always measured, because they are driven by a natural sense of things. I want you to feel this natural sense of things in your mind now. Let your core instincts sharpen your focus, making you more self-assured, more insightful, and more self-aware (Pause). Mother Nature is working with you, and you are working with her. The relationship is harmonious, and peaceful, and it's one that's based on mutual respect. So deeply, deeply relaxed. And while you programme your mind each day with happy thoughts, and positive thoughts, you always remember to instill a happy, and healthy self-image, like you are doing right now (Pause). Relax and flow to your body's natural rhythm. Savour each and every moment of childbirth, knowing it's the most wonderful and exciting experience imaginable. Enjoy moving quickly and deeply into hypnosis. You know the cues, and find that relaxation comes fast when using your out-breath. And the more you breathe, the more you relax, and the more you relax, the better you feel. Relaxing deeper, and deeper still, just letting go, completely. Just allow your subconscious to absorb these important suggestions, and let go now, all the way, drifting deeper, and deeper, deeper, and deeper...

Self-Hypnosis in the Treatment of Irritable Bowel Syndrome

Irritable bowel syndrome, also known as *spastic colon*, is a condition which affects the intestines and bowel. Symptoms of IBS can include cramps, bloating, diarrhea, constipation, heartburn, abdominal pain, excessive gas production, swelling of the abdomen, along with many more uncomfortable symptoms. The reason why self-hypnosis is so successful in helping with IBS is because of the relaxation it brings, which ultimately improves blood flow to the gut. Stress is what inhibits blood flow to the bowel, so the lower your stress levels are, the better your digestion is.

IBS is a complex condition for which there is no known cause. However, most physicians agree that mental and physical factors both trigger its symptoms. Muscular contractions allow food to pass through the stomach and intestines by means of rhythm. With IBS, this natural rhythm is disrupted, resulting in abdominal and intestinal spasms, constipation and diarrhea. The colon has a vast supply of nerves that are connected to the brain called the enteric nervous system. These nerves control the rhythmic contractions of the colon and create abdominal discomfort in stressful times. With IBS, the colon can be overly responsive to even slight stress. So if you are to normalize these contractions, you must first learn to relax your mind.

Certain foods may trigger an attack as the bowel is more sensitive and its symptoms are often aggravated during and after eating. Dairy products, alcohol, caffeine and sugary foods all can irritate the bowel. The sufferer must discover, and often the painful way, which foods to avoid, because they are potential triggers.

Some evidence suggests that the immune system affects IBS, which stress also influences. Hormonal changes may also bring on the condition, but stress will nearly always play a part in its maintenance. Financial pressure would be a typical instigator; a young man/woman with a perfectly healthy digestive system could develop bowel problems on an account of debt. Ulcers could appear under similar circumstances, with continuous stress manifesting itself physically and mentally. Depending on the level of discomfort, a check-up with your doctor is always advised to rule out Crohn's Disease, Ulcerative Colitis, or any other potential illness. Diagnosing IBS is difficult because there is no laboratory test to do so, but its symptoms are not life threatening and should be viewed as such. However, the sufferer has to make strict lifestyle changes with diet, family, work and social life. For some, increasing the amount of fiber in their diet helps to ease the discomfort of constipation. For others it can worsen the condition. What you eat and how much relaxation you get is vital to obtaining relief.

Restoring balance to your thoughts and promoting physical relaxation in your digestive system will keep symptoms of IBS at bay. Avoid stress and keep your energy levels up using the hypnotic techniques that you learn. The energy of your mind protects vulnerable areas like the gut. Stressful environments draw energy away from the body and into the dominant side of the brain, so that we can pay all attention on either fighting or running away from a threat that is usually not present. This can leave bodily organs such as the bowel weak and dysfunctional.

The out-breath is what connects you to the relaxation response. By exhaling slowly, you move energy from the mind back into the body, thus improving blood flow.

Ways to Help IBS

Monitor your diet carefully. Know what you can and cannot eat. Certain foods can help symptoms, e.g. chicken, cod, soya milk, carrots, artichokes, asparagus, bananas, peppermint tea and bio yogurts. But other foods and drinks can trigger symptoms, e.g. red meat, oily, fatty or fried products, coffee, chocolate, sweets and sweeteners.

Eat very slowly and have small, regular meals.

See a doctor and rule out other digestive conditions.

Reduce stress by increasing relaxation and getting plenty of fresh air.

Know that IBS is not life-threatening and believe that your bowels are getting better and better.

Imagine that you are in full control of the problem and pre-empt a future where you are truly free of it. Imagine it, experience it, believe it!

Give yourself post-hypnotic suggestions and cues such as, "Whenever I am out socializing in restaurants, my stomach feels

relaxed, and I feel relaxed." or "Whenever I breathe deeply, the
blood flows to my gut like a waterfall."

Avoid stressful environments and people who drain the energy out
of you.

Use hypnosis to enhance your energy and remove unrealistic fear.

If you are in discomfort or pain, divert attention away from the
problem area by focusing upon an external point as you breathe
deeply. When you sever the connection between fear and
symptom, start giving your mind commands promoting relax-
ation such as, "The more I breathe, the more I relax, and the more
I relax, the better I feel."

Use the rhythm of your breath to normalize the irregular contrac-
tions of your bowel.

Use progressive relaxation to help your mind distinguish between
tension and relaxation. This lets your subconscious know that
you are in control and that you have the power to switch any part
of your body from tension to relaxation whenever you want to.

IBS Script

(Use one of the deepeners from Chapter 5 at the beginning of this script)

Your mind is very sensitive to the words that I am saying to
you. With each day that passes, your body is becoming more and
more relaxed. Trivial matters are easy for you to release, because
now you are looking after your health, and your overall
wellbeing. And the way you feel now, calm, and relaxed, is the
way you are feeling all the time, and in particular, whenever you
are in the presence of food. Food is your friend, and you enjoy
eating all types of delicious food, but you are always careful
about what you eat, and where you eat. Relaxing deeper, and
deeper, so calm, so quiet now (Pause). Inside your body, there is
quietness, and stillness, calmness, and peace. Inside your
digestive system, there is comfort, and perfect relaxation. And
the way that it feels now, is the way it feels all the time. Whenever
you breathe deeply, your entire system automatically relaxes to

the rhythm of your breathing (Pause). You are in full control, always, in full control, of your mind, your body, your emotions, and your feelings, for your mind is perfectly still, and your body, is deeply, deeply, relaxed, so deeply, deeply relaxed, down, down, deeper and deeper (Pause). And while you are sinking into comfort, and tranquillity, realize that you have the power to make those important changes in your body. You are its master, and it is your servant, and you already have the energy to heal your body completely. Just allow this energy that is moving through your mind, just to flow down now, through your face, through your neck, and just feel its energy moving down into your stomach, soothing you within, relaxing you, and healing you. Imagine all the nerves and muscles in your stomach, just settling down now, perfectly, and completely. Allow the energy, that is vibrating in your stomach, just to spread out now, through the rest of your digestive system, relaxing every nerve, every fiber, every cell, soothing you within, relaxing you, and healing you. Imagine the blood flowing freely through your bowels, like little streams and rivers making their way to the sea, flowing calmly, and gently. And as they move along, carrying the blood to where it is needed, there is a pleasant sensation building up inside you, a sensation of energy, and of total relaxation. And whenever you think about your bowels, you imagine a calm, quiet river, blood flowing gently, and energy, protecting your insides. The nerves and muscular contractions of your colon move to a natural, steady rhythm. This rhythm does not change, because you do not change, remaining calm, and relaxed all the time. And whenever you are in stressful situations, its rhythm is perfect (Pause). As your confidence grows stronger and stronger, so too does your digestive system. The way you talk, walk, think and behave, all reflect the confidence that is in you. And because you are taking better care of yourself, it's as though your problem has just faded away to nothing, dissipated into the past, finally, and forever (Pause). Exhale the tension out of your body

223

now (Pause), and again, exhale the tension out of your body (Pause). You are feeling good inside now. And it will be the same in the next moment, and the next hour, and the hours will turn into days, and the days into weeks, and the weeks into months, because now, you are deeply, deeply relaxed. For the next few moments, I will remain silent. I want you to let your mind digest these important suggestions, suggestions that are going to change you, forever.

Chapter 18

Self-Hypnosis for Sport

"The five S's of sports training are: stamina, speed, strength, skill and spirit; but the greatest of these is spirit."
Ken Doherty, Snooker Champion

Getting into the Zone

Self-hypnosis helps the athlete to sharpen focus, increase skill and develop mental and physical strength. Rather than relying on just mere chance, hypnosis brings you naturally and easily into the *zone*; providing energy at the appropriate time and delivering just the right amount. These controlled bursts of energy allow the sportsperson to conserve their strength, minimising effort where it's not needed and maximising power where it is.

The zone is basically a heightened state of awareness, where concentration is total and is uninhibited by internal or external distraction. In the zone, a feeling of time distortion can occur in the mind, slowing down reality enough to anticipate what's coming next, helping you to plan your moves ahead of time. The boxer will see gaps in his opponents defences where he can get through, and the goalkeeper can jump in the right direction as the player is striking the ball. When the mind has grown accoustomed to being in the zone, it will then seek and manifest the same experience everytime you play your game, providing you want, believe and expect it to happen.

With hypnosis, performance preparation can be done in the home as well as on the field. But there's more to sports psychology than just using guided imagery and relaxation techniques. The overall pyschological wellbeing of the athlete must also be considered. Family, social life, work and relationships all can work with or against an athlete. So all aspects of living must be addressed in therapy if you wish to gain insight into what is required to reach your true potential.

Many athletes dedicate a lot of time to improving their physical condition without paying enough attention to their mental needs. They often spend hours on end putting their body through rigorous training, without setting aside fifteen minutes a day to strengthen and focus their mind. This is why some find it harder to move into the zone than others. *Mental conditioning* is what moves you into the zone. But this alteration in perception can only occur when mental interference and distraction have been made practically non-existant. Even if the athlete is surrounded by people and distraction, self-hypnosis can be used to minimize noise, while at the same time increasing focus. The one who uses trance regularly to experience the feeling of being in the zone, can trigger the same response when required, by means of post-hypnotic suggestion, cues, breathing and so on.

Trying too Hard Often Produces Less

Being *too effortful* is one of the main reasons some athletes can't improve their game. Many wonder why they can't go the extra distance and this is often on account of pushing themselves too hard. In an effort to be the best, *force* can sometimes replace *finesse*, resulting in an over-exertion of energy, when all that may be required is a smooth delivery. The tennis player may learn that by loosening their grip a little, power in the wrist can increase while it rests. This way energy can be unleashed at the precise moment it's needed and not a second sooner. This conserving and utilizing of energy is what helps the athlete push harder and go for longer. Getting into the zone via breath, suggestion and imagination, reduces effort while increasing stamina. Slowing down the speed at which the external environment is being perceived in your mind comes about through concentration and controlled breathing. Breathing slowly while fixing your eyes upon objects in the external environment is what helps move you into the zone. By concentrating your attention for moments of engrossed inner focus, you minimize distraction in the mind by narrowing mental and sensory attention to one thing only, the point which you are focusing on. Concentrating intently also helps to prevent your senses from becoming too bombarded by distraction. A suitable place to focus on would be where you wish to go, or where you would your like your javelin or snooker ball to end up. The process needed in order to bring about the end result should be visualized in the imagination during this period of intense concentration. When the subconscious is shown repeated images of how the desired result looks and feels, it can then go about making the body carry out all the necessary actions to make these images real.

Self Confidence: the Vital Necessity

Self-confidence is vital for making sport successful. If you do not believe that you have the ability, then you won't be able to use that ability, no matter how technically skilled you are. Many athletes have the physical strength and capability to go far in their sport, but lack the self-belief that's essential for success. Self-belief often beats technical skill, but when the two are combined, the ultimate athlete is created. The problem with confidence, is that when it gets knocked, it is sometimes hard to recover. This is because confidence takes a good while to build up, but can be taken away in seconds. Self-hypnosis is a great confidence builder and can be used daily to instill images of confidence, intensity, motivation and relaxation. To be the best of the best, you must first imagine that you already are and that success has already been achieved. Confidence is what helps you view your opponent as a challenge to be pursued. When you are confident, you do not view competition as difficult. This is because you have many ways to keep your confidence strong, even when faced with tough opposition or physical injury. Emotional control is what helps successful athletes see with clarity.

Intensity: Using it Wisely

In many sports, how the athlete controls their mental and physical levels of intensity is crucial in learning how to optimize performance. *Positive intensity* results in confidence, motivation, brain and muscular stimulation, strength and endurance. *Negative intensity* can result from a lack in confidence and motivation, poor brain and muscular stimulation, fatigue, difficulty breathing, etc. Intensity ranges from being very calm and relaxed while engaged in sport, to breaking the pain barrier through extreme mental, physical and environmental conditions. By noticing the times you are short of breath, or when you experience tightness in your muscles, you can identify what is causing over-intensity and make the necessary changes to stop it. Over-intensity has a negative effect upon health and sport, but by learning to control intensity, stamina is accelerated, helping the athlete to break through mental and physical barriers.

The Emotional Athlete

The emotional wellbeing of the athlete is of paramount importance. Not enough emphasis is placed on the role that emotions play in sport, but in order for you to be on top of your game, you must be in charge of your emotions. In the same way you switch off from your critical conscious mind in hypnosis, so too can you by-pass the distraction of thought and emotion by using hypnosis to get into the zone. Learning to put your emotions aside takes time to master. But a good way to start is by first taking charge of your emotional needs. The more you are in control of your emotions, the less you have to distract yourself from them while performing. The process of removing psychological and emotional barriers involves identifying them, understanding their meaning and then making the necessary changes to minimize their impact on your sport. Emotions when used productively can improve your game. An example of this would be an athlete winning a competition shortly after hearing his wife has just giving birth. Such a life changing experience would inspire and motivate a person to win, in the same way a death in the family could have the same or opposite effect.

Goal-Setting to Enhance Your Game

Setting goals to be achieved in lifestyle, diet, training, competition, etc. can be implanted each day in hypnosis. If you are using a coach or sports consultant, they too must understand how the goal-setting process works and how best to apply goals that suit your individual needs. Setting goals not only involves achieving outcomes within your sport, it also includes setting and achieving goals within your personal life. It could be difficult for an athlete to win gold in the olympics if their marraige was in a crisis. This is because life and sport do not work in isolation. It is why goal-setting should always be geared towards achieving harmony both on and off the field.

Using Imagery to Enhance Your Game

As you have already learned, imagery (also called visualization or mental rehearsal) is a technique for programming your subconscious to respond in a certain way. It involves using the five senses to create the desired experience in your imagination before it has actually happened. It is a mental workout that approximates reality, because all that is missing from the picture is the motor response of the muscles. By imagining a previous experience of winning, you can program your mind to expect the same by focusing on these images in hypnosis.

Imagery can be used before and during rehearsal and competition. The tennis player may spend fifteen minutes in mental rehearsal before a big match, visualizing a perfect performance, set by set. Just before they serve, imagery can again be used to pin-point exactly where the ball is going to land.

Imagery is where you think in images instead of words. By allowing perception to become more visual, you are less distracted by thoughts that often interfere in the form of words. Paying close attention to detail in your imaginings helps increase the likelihood of your subconscious carrying out your intentions in reality, as does adding rich colour or feeling the cricket bat in your hand.

Some athletes get nervous purely on account of the crowd capacity where they are performing. By imagining the crowd supporting you, and what these people will look and sound like, unrealistic fear can be significantly reduced on the day of the big event through self-hypnosis. When imagining, it's important to see events unfolding as if you are looking through your own eyes, rather than observing yourself from a distance. Feel the feelings that come with being in the zone, even if this means imagining sweat on your body. See yourself in full flight, exerting just the right amount of intensity, at just the right time. See the end result, hear the crowd erupting and feel the trophy in your hand. The more senses you involve, the more instilled these images become in your subconscious. Repeating the same images daily in hypnosis will keep your program positive and up-to-date.

Post-hypnotic suggestions and cues will help maintain confidence, motivation and focus. Here are some examples of the type of post-hypnotic suggestions you can use:

"The sound of the crowd relaxes me deeply."
"The more I run, the more energy I feel."
"When I breathe deeply, I automatically concentrate."
"Each time I train, I get better and better."
"The tougher the opposition, the stronger I become."

The Benefits of Using Self-Hypnosis in Sport

Improved confidence, motivation, stamina, mind-body connection, focus, perception, intensity, energy, self-control, self-discipline, self-awareness, physical strength, time management, balance between work, family, social and sport life.

Faster recuperation and recovery time.

Ability to control pain.

The ability to get into the zone quickly and easily.

By mentally rehearsing training and competition in hypnosis, you significantly increase the likihood of achieving your goals in reality.

In the same way breath, suggestion, imagination, concentration, belief and expectancy are central to hypnosis, so too are they central to sport. It's all about preparation, and what better way to prepare than to relax in trance each day.

Hypnosis can be used to generate desire and interest, where the incentive to train or compete may be lacking.

By looking after your emotional needs, you are looking after your sporting needs.

Hypnosis provides such a platform for emotional healing to take place, where anxiety, worry, and stress can be reduced or removed.

Hypnosis keeps the digestive system relaxed and stress-free. This is important to the athlete whose diet can sometimes be very strict. Certain protein enriched foods can irritate the bowel, but stress will almost certainly aggrivate an existing problem.

Hypnosis brings all the appropriate muscles into play, so that outbursts of energy are channelled into the right areas of the body.

When you visualize making a perfect movement or action, the muscles needed to accomplish that action begin moving in the correct way. With practice, these mentally rehearsed movements are easily transferred to the tennis court, golf course, swimming pool and so on.

When concentration and relaxation are total, the mind naturally slips into a heightened state of awareness. This is what gives certain athletes the edge over others. While many people use concentration and relaxation techniques to improve their game, few use their mental abilities to quite the same degree as those practicing self-hypnosis.

Mental Training for Mental Toughness

Mental training should cover a wide variety of skills and not be restricted to performance preparation and competition. Conditioning the mind involves getting the most out of training sessions, dealing with setbacks, recovering from injury, combating fatigue and coping with sickness and frustration. A strong mind can help the body recover quicker, so by staying mental fit, you stay physically fit also.

For the athlete approaching a big event they are not yet mentally prepared for, a lack in self-belief could give rise to psychosomatic symptoms, such as poor concentration, cramps or injury. The subconscious must be convinced that there's nothing to fear and that competition is a challange to be pursued and won. If it has not been convinced, it may then attempt to sabotage the athletes plans by creating barriers in an effort to keep them away from the event. This act of *sabotage* happens at a subconscious level, and so, must be rectified there too. Hypnosis has been proven a useful tool for overcoming such mental obstacles, because it paints a clear picture in the subconscious of what success looks and feels like, and how it should be replicated into reality. By removing unrealistic fear and bolstering your belief system, you automatically begin increasing self-confidence, possibly the most essential component for achieving success in sport.

Sports Psychology Script

(Use one of the deepeners from Chapter 5 at the beginning of this script)

So as you continue to drift deeper, you can feel awareness growing within you, a certainty that you have the ability, the confidence, and the determination that is required to excel at your sport. Because you have shed your limitations, you are capable of remaining in full control, and this gives you the courage to push harder. You know that whenever you put your mind to something, you always achieve it. This is the real you (Pause) sharp, focused, committed, prepared, energized, the one who is on top of their game, because you work hard, and enjoy the preparation, the competition, because it relaxes you, and stimulates your creative mind. And the more you breathe, the more you relax, and the more you relax, the better you feel, relaxing deeper, and deeper still, just letting go, completely (Pause). At this very moment, every part of you is being cleansed, purified, and revitalized. And as your concentration and relaxation allows your body's healing processes to be active, you find yourself developing a sense of strength and confidence, strength and confidence, growing stronger, and stronger, stronger, and stronger. Through relaxation, your peace of mind and inner serenity grows, enabling you to cope well with any stresses that may arise. People, situations and things that used to interfere with your sport, now calm you, and whenever you think of those people, situations and things that used to upset you, they serve to relax you further, relaxing further and further, deeper and deeper, further and further, deeper and deeper (Pause). Each day you notice improvements in the fitness of your body, and you also notice how this fitness and vitality brings with it feelings of pleasure and achievement to your mind. As time passes, your body feels more and more healthy, fitter and fitter, healthier and healthier, fitter and fitter. The fitness and wellbeing that you feel in your sport is determined by you, and you alone. This is why you make time each day to relax and use your imagination. And when you imagine, you always visualize the perfect performance. This is because sport comes naturally to you, and is second nature to you, and because it is second nature to you, you do not have to try too hard, for winning is something you do easily, and effortlessly. Now, more than ever, you are extremely focused, determined and committed; committed to your sport, your health, and your lifestyle in general. You take sport seriously, because it is an essential part of your activites, but more importantly, you enjoy all that it has to offer, in terms of fitness, pleasure, excitement, and sociability. And when you are training, or in competition, you find that you are very relaxed throughout, and because you are always so relaxed, it shows on your face, and in your actions. Whenever the need arises, you are able to calm yourself down, by focusing in on your breath. This is because you realise the importance of using your breath in a controlled manner, knowing that every time you breathe diaphramatically, you automatically become focused (Pause). Getting into the zone via breath, suggestion, and imagination, reduces effort while increasing stamina. This is your time, your time to show the world what you are capable of, what you were born to do, what you can achieve when you put your mind to it. Your subconscious is now making the necessary changes to make you a winner, to make you the best of the best. Now it is making these suggestions a permanent part of your thinking.

Conclusion

By now you should be more proficient at inducing the hypnotic state, with a clear understanding of how best to reprogram the way you think, feel and behave. Having grasped the basic but necessary requirements for achieving self-mastery, your journey must now continue by participating regularly in mind-challenging activities and self-hypnotic relaxation. Action is what keeps your mind and body stress free, and relaxation is what charges up the energy for the action to happen.

Think of your subconscious as a busy computer, and be on guard for the occasional virus. Breath, suggestion and imagination are your anti-viruses. Whenever you feel off-line, I want you to switch to simple, present tense auto-suggestion, and regain control by taking the necessary time out to breathe and relax. Even just fifteen minutes a day in trance makes a significant difference to your overall mental and physical wellbeing.

Mind and body are as one, with imagination at the helm. It has the ability to create good health as well as ill-health and must be used actively; otherwise it becomes counter-productive, with too much reliance on will power alone. Bright, colorful images drive your mind forward with purpose and destiny. By mapping out the voyage beforehand using visual preparation, you significantly decrease the likelihood of getting lost at sea. It is fear which stops you from moving into uncharted waters; fear which springs from your subconscious when left to its own devices. Consistently replacing negative images with positive, desired ones, is an ongoing mental exercise you must engage in.

Find your safe place, somewhere quiet to relax. Locate a point to focus on while you breathe. After a short time allow your eyes to gently close. Brief moments of engrossed inner focus like this enable your conscious mind to power down and regenerate energy. It also encourages heightened awareness by slowing reality down enough to normalize your perception of it. You should invest in quality time like this regularly rather than firing on all cylinders without respite; which inevitably leads to mental exhaustion and bodily stresses.

Staying positive and healthy is about dealing appropriately with the negative. You can avoid slipping back into old ways by *spot-checking* your thoughts and feelings for sabotaging behavior. Negative people give in to sabotage easily and crumble when faced with the inevitable setback. But by recognizing sabotage when it appears, you stick to the game plan, which is dealing appropriately with the negative through action. Follow your core feelings, your instincts, as they guide you. You already know the answers to many of life's questions, but self-sabotage sometimes results in either ignoring the solutions or putting them on hold. Positive thinking is a state of mind, which manifests to the full when combined with *self-belief*.

Encourage and give yourself credit where credit is due. Do not berate yourself when you make a mistake. This only serves to help you make the same mistakes again. If there is trauma from the past affecting you, consult a healthcare professional immediately, and spend some valuable time in therapy. Combining professional help with this book is a good way to yield positive results. However, if you currently suffer with your mental or physical health, please, make an appointment today! Most problems are best dealt through professional treatment and support.

Some things in life are instantly likeable, but there are other things you acquire a taste for. Self-hypnosis helps you to develop new tastes, providing of course you expose your pallet to all the wonderful flavors that make up the entire dish that is life. Stepping forward into the unknown enlightens a fearful subconscious to be brave and independent in the face of uncertainty. It also accelerates the pulse of life, so that desired goals are achieved more spontaneously. By moving with the pulse and rhythm of life, it then becomes an adventure.

Get to know who you are, what makes you tick. Change the things you don't like about yourself. You must break the monotony of routine if you wish to successfully re-write the program that currently runs inside your mind!

In order to satisfy needs without alcohol, drugs, or other harmful substances, old habits must be substituted with new, healthier ones. Moderation is self-control, for it sets limitations on that which is occasional. Indulging too much in life's pleasures gives your subconscious little to strive for; as it only encourages energy to move inwards in search of happiness, which isn't always there, especially if you are in the midst of addiction.

If you are suffering from an addiction, use self-hypnosis, but seek professional help as well. Rid yourself of it once and for all. The only way to truly put an end to addiction is to avoid participating in it. Bury your problem in the past and move on. Thousands have done so and continue to do with help from their families, friends and support groups.

Watch out for those who demand too much of your time and energy. Be a good listener without having the life sucked out of you by the needy. It takes a little practice, especially if you are gentle person of a quiet disposition. How you identify the energy suckers is by spot-checking whether your energy levels feel low or high during and after conversing with them. If you feel drained, well, then you'll know to spend less time in future with them. If on the other hand you are full to the brim with energy, that is good, but make sure it is because the flow of conversation is equal and not because you are the one absorbing all the energy.

Energy and desire create natural sensations of balance and harmony while engaging in healthy activities. Paradoxically, they also create sensations of imbalance and disharmony when invested in unhealthy activities. If you wish to be free from your symptoms, your subconscious must first learn that it does not have to invest energy in that which is counter-productive. This is best done with professional help.

Becoming the product of your own desire is positive and healthy, but it means taking command of your subconscious program by enriching it daily with carefully chosen words, images, thoughts and feelings. By observing and correcting your internal dialogue and the manner in which you speak to yourself, misinformation is then replaced with truth. This enables you to remain free of self-punishing language and sabotaging behaviour. Be kind to yourself. It's important and crucial to wellbeing.

You have the necessary tools for achieving self-mastery, positive health, success and happiness. Now I want to wish you every success in fulfilling your dreams. You know what positive changes you want, but only you can make them happen, so go ahead and make them happen. Use the wonderful mind you have been blessed with and let nothing stand in your way. Learn to listen, follow your senses, stay in control, use your imagination, toughen up, do not give in, forgive and forget, be original, repeat positive suggestions, give others a second chance, trust your intuition, control your anger, respect your food, be imperfect, take the scenic route, find a new hobby, watch less television, care for all living things, loosen up, don't worry, commit to your goals, don't hold a grudge, keep it simple, see problems as solutions, open your mind, but most important of all... breathe. Good luck!

Further Reading

I highly recommend *The Art of Hypnosis* by famous hypnotherapist Roy Hunter.

An Invitation

Cathal O'Briain gives lectures, seminars and workshops all over Ireland and overseas. For further details, dates and information please see his website www.hypnosis.ie

Cathal O'Briain
81 Beatty Park
Maynooth Road
Celbridge
Co. Kildare
Ireland
Tel 0035316279397
cathal@hypnosis.ie
www.powerfulmindhypnosis.com

Sources

Oxford Dictionary.

The Archives of the Institute of Clinical Hypnotherapy and Psychotherapy (Ireland).

Permission from Roy Hunter to quote Charles Tebbets and Ormond Gill.

Upshaw, W.N (2006) *Medicine's Dirty Word,* American Journal of Clinical Hypnosis.

Goldberg, B (2005) *Secrets of Hypnosis,* Sterling Publishing Company.

MacKenzie, R (2005) *Self-Change Hypnosis,* Trafford Publishing.

O'Brien, D (2004) *History of Ericksonian Hypnosis,* Healthmap Magazine.

Jung, C.G (1916) *Psychology of the Unconscious,* Princeton University Press.

Fink, B (1999) *A Clinical Introduction to Lacanian Psychoanalysis,* Harvard University Press.

Websites

http://mysite.verizon.net/jim2wr/id85.html

http://findarticles.com/p/articles/mi_qa4087/is_200610/ai_n17194
408/pg_2

http://findarticles.com/p/articles/mi_qa4087/is_200610/ai_n17194
408/pg_2

http://findarticles.com/p/articles/mi_qa4087/is_200610/ai_n17194
408/pg_2

http://findarticles.com/p/articles/mi_qa4087/is_200610/ai_n17194
408/pg_3

http://findarticles.com/p/articles/mi_qa4087/is_200610/ai_n17194
408/pg_3

http://findarticles.com/p/articles/mi_qa4087/is_200610/ai_n17194
408/pg_3

http://findarticles.com/p/articles/mi_qa4087/is_200610/ai_n17194
408/pg_4

http://findarticles.com/p/articles/mi_qa4087/is_200610/ai_n17194
408/pg_4

http://findarticles.com/p/articles/mi_qa4087/is_200610/ai_n17194
408/pg_4

http://findarticles.com/p/articles/mi_qa4087/is_200610/ai_n17194
408/pg_5

http://www.ericksonian.com/Milton-erickson.html

http://en.wikipedia.org/wiki/History_of_hypnosis#Dave_Elman

http://www.drjackgibson.com/biography.html

http://www.richardmackenzie.co.uk/history.htm

http://www.quoteworld.org/quotes/10320

http://www.mdhypnosis.com/quit-smoking.htm

www.thinkexist.com

B O O K S

O is a symbol of the world, of oneness and unity. In different cultures it also means the "eye," symbolizing knowledge and insight. We aim to publish books that are accessible, constructive and that challenge accepted opinion, both that of academia and the "moral majority."

Our books are available in all good English language bookstores worldwide. If you don't see the book on the shelves ask the bookstore to order it for you, quoting the ISBN number and title. Alternatively you can order online (all major online retail sites carry our titles) or contact the distributor in the relevant country, listed on the copyright page.

See our website **www.o-books.net** for a full list of over 500 titles, growing by 100 a year.

And tune in to myspiritradio.com for our book review radio show, hosted by June-Elleni Laine, where you can listen to the authors discussing their books.

MySpiritRadio